Essays on German History and Historians

To Bill & Ursula
old and cherished
friends.

Jim

Essays on German History and Historians

James J. Sheehan

The Society for the Promotion of Science and Scholarship
Palo Alto, California

The Society for the Promotion of Science and Scholarship
Palo Alto, California

© 2022 The Society for the Promotion of Science and
Scholarship, Inc.

The Society for the Promotion of Science and Scholarship is a
nonprofit organization established for the purposes of
scholarly publishing, to benefit both academics and the general
public. It has special interests in European and British studies.

Published with the assistance of a gift from Larry N. Horton

Printed in the United States of America

ISBN cloth: 978-0-930664-33-6
ISBN paper: 978-0-930664-34-3

To Renate Wehler and Ruth Becker

And in loving memory of Uli Wehler and Josef Becker

Contents

Preface   ix

1. Living in History: An Autobiographical Introduction   1

Part I: In Search of a Subject

2. What is German History? Reflections on the Role of the
   Nation in German History and Historiography   19

3. The Problem of the Nation in German History   51

4. National History and National Identity in the
   New Germany   75

5. Paradigm Lost? The Sonderweg Revisited   92

Part II: German Historians, Historians of Germany

6. Three Generations of German Gelehrtenpolitik   109

7. The Primacy of Domestic Politics: Eckart Kehr's
   Essays on Modern German History   117

8. Mack Walker's *German Home Towns*   129

9. Carl Schorske at Berkeley   135

10. Saul Friedländer   139

11. Gordon A. Craig   142

12. Werner Thomas Angress   149

13. Hans-Ulrich Wehler   153

14. Gerhard A. Ritter   160

15. Fritz Stern   165

Conclusion

16. The Future of the German Past   171

Index   181

Preface

Although these essays were written between 1968 and 2017, they were all shaped by my experiences in the second half of the twentieth century. For historians of Germany, two events dominated our perception of this period. One was the legacy of National Socialism, which left an enduring imprint on German politics, culture, and society. The other was the Cold War between the United States and the Soviet Union, which began, and in some sense, ended in German-speaking Central Europe. Together these two complex phenomena shaped our understanding of both the German past and the German present. And while neither disappeared after 1989, the end of the European Cold War and the unification of the two postwar German states did mark the beginning of a new chapter in the long history of the "German Question."

Because the essays in Part I reflect both the scholarship and the political assumptions of the postwar period, many of them are out of date. If I were to address these subjects today, at the beginning of the twenty-first century's third decade, I would do so very differently. I have, nevertheless, resisted the temptation to revise the texts and the even greater temptation to add more recent literature to the notes. While this may undermine the essays' value as commentaries on the past, it may (or at least so I hope) enhance their value as reflections of the present in which they were written.

Part II is about scholars of German history, most of whom were my teachers, mentors, colleagues, and friends. They have all played an important part in shaping our view of Germany's past. I hope it will be clear how much the scholarly world, and I personally, benefited from their work. Writing about these historians was, and remains, a modest acknowledgment of the immense debt I owe them.

Speaking of debts, I have also incurred more than my share of them in the preparation of this volume. My old friend and colleague, Peter Stansky, encouraged me to collect these essays; it is fair to say that without him, this book would not exist. Isser Woloch was kind enough to read a draft and make some characteristically acute suggestions. Elena Kempf did excellent work tidying up the manuscript. Norris Pope played a critically important part in the production process. Not for the first time (nor, I devoutly hope, for the last), Michael Sheehan provided prompt, efficient, and resolutely cheerful technical assistance. Finally, Peggy Anderson, the historian in the room next to mine, enhanced the author's life in more ways than this brief preface can describe. Among the many things for which I have reason to be grateful, she is at the top of the list.

James J. Sheehan, March 2022

Essays on German History and Historians

Living in History:
An Autobiographical Introduction[*]

"Living in History"—the title illustrates my long-held belief that the most complex word in any title is usually the shortest. In this case, of course, that word is <u>in</u>, which has at least two meanings. First, living in history makes the obvious point that, as a historian, I have spent a large part of my time living in the past, studying events that happened long ago, trying to understand men and women who are long dead, fighting battles that have already been lost or won. But living in history also refers to the fact that like everyone else, I live in a present that will eventually become the past and is therefore part of history. The great Swiss historian Jacob Burckhardt captured the distinctive difficulty of understanding this second sort of living in history with a memorable metaphor: "We would," he wrote, "love to know the wave that carries us on the ocean, but we ourselves are the wave."

These two ways of living in history are obviously inseparable since our efforts to understand the past, that is, to understand how things were then and there, are always done in the present, in the here and now.

This afternoon I would like to share some tentative reflections on these two ways of living in history (and on the

[*]Revised version of a talk given to the Stanford Emeriti Council, February 2017.

connection between them). I should say at once that I will not talk about my private history: this is not because love, marriage, parenthood, and friendship were and are not important to me—quite the opposite is true, indeed these things are so important, so close to my heart, that I simply cannot find the voice to talk about them in a forum like this one. Instead, I will offer you what the Germans would call a Bildungsroman, a novel of education in which the protagonist—often, as in the present case, a young man from the provinces—confronts a number of situations and individuals that eventually help him find his place in the world.

Where to begin? David Abernethy suggested that many of my distinguished predecessors in this series have talked about the importance of some early experience on their development as scholars, a childhood interest perhaps, or a particularly inspiring grade school teacher. Now I had my share—perhaps more than my share—of good teachers and I have no doubt that my childhood influenced me in many significant ways, but I must confess that neither had much to do with the subjects to which I have devoted my scholarly life. My parents had very little interest in history in general and absolutely no interest in the European past. Irish history, the nightmare that haunted James Joyce's Stephan Daedalus, did not haunt us. The European experience seemed very far away from California where, for white people anyway, historical identities were present, but remained rather weak, probably because they were not enforced by the ethnic rivalries that were so important in other parts of the United States. Similarly, the Catholic Church, the moral center of my family's existence, was at once profoundly traditional and oddly unhistorical or, it might be better to say, remarkably unaware of the historical forces that had shaped its character. These forces came to the surface only in the 1960s when the character of the church began to be transformed by the Second Vatican Council. My boyhood was spent in a pre-Vatican Two church that was self-confident, affluent, and firmly fixed in the present. In my Jesuit High

School, the level of instruction was high: Latin, as one might expect, was well taught, as were (perhaps less predictably) Chemistry and Physics; I had a wonderful English teacher in my senior year; but history was left in the not very capable hands of the football and basketball coaches. The closest I can come to locating an early influence on my interest in history was an uncle who collected books about the American West and had a special interest in George Armstrong Custer. At one point I knew a lot about the passionate debates over what really happened on the Little Big Horn river in June 1876—Custer's Last Stand was the first, and for many years the only, historiographical controversy to capture my attention.

Looking back, I now think that what would fascinate me about Europe and especially about Germany—that is, the histories in and from which I have lived—is how different they were from the peaceful, prosperous, and provincial world of Irish Catholic San Francisco in which three generations of my family had lived. When I first went to Germany in 1961—this was, as you may recall, the year the Berlin Wall was built and Adolf Eichmann was put on trial in Jerusalem—I found myself for the first time in a place where the past was ever present. Even sixteen years after the end of the Third Reich, people were constantly aware of living in and with history.

Before talking about my relationship with Germany, I suppose I have to say a few words about my four years as a student at Stanford—although I must admit that it was a happy day when I realized that no one would ever have to look at my undergraduate transcript again. Tocqueville once remarked that America had the privilege of making survivable mistakes—and in that way, to paraphrase the Jacques Brel song, Stanford was like America for me.

Stanford in the fifties was just beginning its remarkable climb to world-class status. In many ways the university I entered as a freshman in 1954 was a different institution from the one to which I would return as a faculty member a quarter of a century later. Nevertheless then (as now), it was a deeply tolerant, rather loosely knit place, with lots of quite distinct student subcultures. Then (and I suspect that this may still the case) it was possible to get a very fine education, in part because a number of undergraduates didn't particularly want one. I am afraid that I belonged to this group until sometime in my junior year when, for reasons I can't identify, I decided to begin taking advantage of the extraordinary opportunities available to me. In acting on this newly found sense of purpose and direction, two teachers were especially important for my future.

The first was Donald Davidson, one of the twentieth century's most important and influential philosophers, who taught a wonderful course on ethics in which he critically examined a series of classical texts. I had previously taken several philosophy courses, but Davidson's was uniquely challenging and inspiring. It was also instructive in another way, because I left his lectures convinced that while I could understand and appreciate what he was doing, I would never be able to match it. I could be—and would remain—an avid consumer of philosophical texts, but I would never produce one of my own. Years later I met Davidson at a dinner party in Berkeley and told him that he was one of the few teachers who had changed my life. I didn't say how, nor, I must admit, did he seem especially interested in finding out.

My other influential undergraduate teacher was Gordon Wright, who had joined Stanford's History Department when I was a senior. I took his course on modern France, a beautifully crafted set of lectures that remains for me the gold standard for what a history course should be. More important, I persuaded Gordon to give me a course of directed readings, a tutorial in which we met for an hour each week to talk about a book. This was, I now realize, an incredibly (and I should add, characteristically) generous thing for him to do. It introduced me to a world of intellectual exchange that I found thrilling: what could be more satisfying than talking to a very smart and learned person about good books on important subjects? If this is what historians got paid to do, this might be for me. The prospect of Law School—which had become for me, as for so many undecided humanities students, a potential harbor in which to escape the stormy sea of post-graduation uncertainty—faded and instead, haphazardly and at the last minute, I applied to some doctoral programs in history.

I do not want to overstate the strength of my vocation to be a historian, nor to underestimate my ignorance about what this would involve. Under different circumstances I might have taken a year off to think about my future—which is certainly what I have often advised students in a similar state to do. But in 1958 the Selective Service Law effectively precluded that option. The choice was between going to graduate school or spending two years in the army, performing peacetime duties which, according to my friends who had been drafted, turned out to involve long periods of boredom punctuated by occasional humiliations—which sounded to me rather like a two-year softball game. In any case, I decided to accept U.C. Berkeley's offer of admission to its doctoral program. This decision—taken with some reluctance and in almost total obliviousness about its implications—turned out to be one that I have never for a single moment regretted.

It was a sign of my quite appalling ignorance of what graduate school might be like that I was shocked and surprised when, early in the summer after graduation, I received a letter from the Director of Graduate Studies informing me that, while I had been accepted into Berkeley's doctoral program, before I could enroll in any graduate level courses I would have to pass an examination demonstrating my proficiency in a foreign language. This presented a serious problem. I had studied Latin and Greek in High School (the only languages then offered at St Ignatius) and while my Latin had once been fairly good, it was now rusty—and in any case, I knew that Ancient History would not be my primary interest. This meant that if I were to make a remotely plausible claim to competence it would have to be in German, the language I had studied—if that is the verb to describe my academic deportment in those days—during my first two years at Stanford.

That I had decided to study German—perhaps the single most consequential academic decision I would make as an undergraduate—was the result of a piece of advice from a man married to one of my cousins whose father had studied medicine in Vienna before the First World War. My cousin's husband, a successful physician in San Francisco, continued to believe that because German was the language of science it would surely enhance what my family then hoped would be my own medical career. This piece of wisdom was, of course, about a half century out of date. I used to think that it was fairly comical that my scholarly interests should have begun this way. But now I recognize that my decision to study German was a belated instance of Germany's enormous influence on American academic life—it just took a while for this influence to find its way to the Sheehan household in the fog bound precincts of St Francis Woods.

That summer, to perform the pedagogical equivalent of CPR on my linguistic skills, I engaged a tutor: Frau Strauss, a widow of a certain age, who provided me with bad coffee, stale cookies, and briskly efficient language instruction. I learned more German during the hours I spent in her Berkeley apartment than I had in six quarters at Stanford. This was the opening skirmish in what would turn out to be my long twilight struggle with the German language, which I eventually learned to speak like a native—but not, alas, a native of Germany. Frau Strauss was also the first representative of a group of people who would play an immensely important part in my Bildungsroman: refugees from Hitler's Germany, who brought their language, culture, and history to the United States. Several of them will appear in what follows.

Thanks in no small part to the efforts of Frau Strauss, I managed to pass the necessary language exam and so was able to enroll in a graduate research seminar on nineteenth-century German history. The teacher was Werner Angress, called Tom by his friends, another refugee. Tom had grown up in an assimilated Jewish family in Berlin. They fled to the Netherlands after Hitler came to power; Tom's father returned to Germany briefly in 1939, was trapped there when the war began, and died in Auschwitz; his mother and two brothers survived the war hiding in Amsterdam, while Tom managed to get to the United States where he was promptly drafted. Small in stature and rather cherubic in appearance, he turned out to be a tough and effective soldier (he parachuted into France on D-Day; it was his first jump). All of this, by the way, I found out much later: Tom was not someone to let his own story intrude on the serious enterprise of historical research.

Tom was warm-hearted and kind, but he was also a demanding and extraordinarily conscientious teacher. Many years later, while we were having dinner together in Berlin (to which he had returned after his retirement), he told me that he had just reread the paper I wrote for his seminar and decided that he should not have given me a B+; I had surely deserved an A-. I am not at all sure he was right, but I am sure that he was deeply concerned that he had, a half century earlier, treated me unjustly.

Although I was totally unaware of it when I applied, in the late fifties Berkeley was in the process of becoming one of the world's greatest history departments, with particular strength in the history of Europe, the area to which my shaky claim to competence in German had brought me. (You have, I hope, already noticed what a large role blind luck plays in this story.) When I arrived in the fall of 1958, the leading European historian was Raymond J. Sontag, a formidable figure, charismatic lecturer, and, to me at least, an extraordinarily generous mentor. Like most great teachers, Ray Sontag's influence came less from what he taught than from who he was: during the two years I spent as his teaching and then research assistant, I learned a lot of history, but, much more important, by observing the way he went about his work and how he lived his life, I began to learn what it meant to be a historian.

Two other senior scholars, both hired about the time I entered the program, were also important for my time at Berkeley. One was Carl Schorske, the author of a brilliant study of German Social Democracy, who was beginning to work on what would become a series of essays on fin de siècle Vienna for which he would win a Pulitzer Prize in 1981. Carl, who died last year at 100, had one of those incandescent intelligences that illuminates every subject it examines. He also had the ability of inspiring without intimidating, of making even an ill-prepared novice feel like he was a companion on a shared intellectual journey.

Hans Rosenberg, the second Berkeley historian to leave a lasting mark on my life, was both inspiring and intimidating. He was the only teacher I ever saw who could reduce a grown man to tears, not by being cruel but simply by turning the full force of his critical intelligence on the student's efforts. Rosenberg (I eventually brought myself to call him Hans, but never, I must say, with much confidence or conviction—in any case, as a friend of mine once said, it didn't matter what I called him, he always knew he was Professor Rosenberg) was a student of Friedrich Meinecke, a great German historian who had attracted many gifted young scholars to the University of Berlin in the late twenties. Even in this stellar group, Rosenberg had stood out: he published two books and a score of important articles by the time he was thirty. A Jew (at least by the Nazis' definition) and a left-leaning defender of the Weimar Republic, there was, needless to say, no place for him in Hitler's Germany. His brilliant career cruelly interrupted, he fled, first to England and then the United States where he taught at Brooklyn College before finally moving to Berkeley. The road from his precociously promising beginning in Meinecke's seminar to the endowed chair in Berkeley was long and arduous: without private means, struggling with a language he never quite mastered, burdened with heavy teaching responsibilities, he published relatively little for two decades. Yet he never gave up and by the time I met him in 1959, his work had begun to exert enormous influence, especially over a new generation of historians in West Germany.

Rosenberg and, somewhat later his fellow Berlin student, Felix Gilbert, were the two members of the émigré generation who were most important for me. It is, I think, impossible to overestimate the significance of this group of exiled artists and scholars for American intellectual life in the middle decades of the twentieth century: I suspect that many of you, if you reflect for a moment about the recent history of your disciplines, will find that German refugees had had a profound influence.

For American students of European history, émigré scholars like Rosenberg and Gilbert were role models for at least three reasons.

First was their erudition, by which I mean not simply their remarkable command of the sources and secondary literature, but also that distinctive blend of learning and cultivation that marked them as intellectuals and personalities.

Second was their cosmopolitanism, by which I mean not simply the breadth of their experiences but also the breadth of their sympathies, which had enabled them to embrace the new world into which fate had thrust them without losing their old attachments. This is a complicated matter about which a great deal more might be said, but it surely has something to do with the fact that they were assimilated German Jews, who had been shaped by a national culture to which they were deeply committed and yet from which they were necessarily separated. Their cosmopolitanism was not a pious sentiment, but a hard-won reckoning with complex loyalties. Even for the best adjusted of them, this was not without its costs. But it was exemplary to young American students like me, who were voluntarily setting out to live in a historical world that was not our own.

Finally, there was the way they personified living in history. All of them had, to some degree, felt Nazism's foul breadth on the back of their necks: whether they talked about it or not, this gave their work an undeniable moral urgency and purpose. Despite the pains of emigration and the burden of advancing years, they all kept on working and as such they were living testimonies to the enduring value of the scholar's vocation. In their presence no one could doubt that history mattered. More than anything else, this was their most precious gift to me and it is the one for which I am most grateful.

The émigrés provided a transatlantic connection in another important way by introducing young Americans like myself to the new generation of German scholars who were just then beginning to establish their careers and make their mark on the discipline. These people—almost all of them men—were slightly older than I, born in the early rather than the late 1930s. They belonged to the Hitler Youth generation, too young to be active participants in Nazism's crimes, but old enough to know that, if the regime had lasted just a little longer, they would have been deeply involved. They were also the exchange student generation, many of whom had come to the United States in the 1950s and were decisively influenced by what seemed—and in some ways was—a vibrant, prosperous, self-confident democracy. I was fortunate indeed to be able to forge bonds of friendship with several of these German scholars, who taught me a great deal and enriched my life in ways too numerous to mention.

Intellectually, all of us were engaged in trying to understand the German question, that is, a cluster of questions about the origins and character of National Socialism. Initially, the most important dimension of the German question seemed to be the collapse of German democracy at the end of the Weimar Republic, a matter of obvious importance as Germans set out to create a new democratic regime amid the ruins—physical, political, and moral—left in the wake of Nazism's defeat. By the time I became a serious student of German history, the emphasis had begun to shift from the immediate to the long run problems of German democracy: the issue now was to trace the roots of the Nazi catastrophe back into the German past, especially into the nineteenth century. What was it about Germany's development that produced a series of political calamities that culminated in 1933? Why had Germany deviated so sharply and tragically from the West? In other words, why did Germans' route to modernity follow a special path, a Sonderweg that led them to catastrophe?

Many of you will recognize that the way we posed his question was shaped by a series of assumptions about the nature of modernization, assumptions that were part of that grand narrative of historical change—conventionally called modernization theory—that dominated American social science in the postwar era. Not surprisingly, this approach to the German past was very much a transatlantic project: among its earlier and most influential protagonists had been members of the émigré generation and among its most devoted practitioners were the young scholars who had spent a formative year or two as exchange students in the United States.

The effort to define and explain the German Sonderweg, Germany's separate, deviant path to modernity, was what the historian of science Thomas Kuhn called a paradigm: that is, a set of assumptions that provide a consensus about the questions that need to be posed and a framework for the inevitable disagreements that arose about how these questions should be answered—in other words, that mixture of consensus and conflict on which every discipline depends. As Kuhn noted, one of the sources of a paradigm's influence was its ability to generate research problems, empirical puzzles that Kuhn called "normal science." In the case of the Sonderweg, many of these research problems had to do with apparent absences, things Germans did not have that the "West" supposedly did—an authentic revolution, a politically self-conscious middle class, a critical intellectual elite—or with failures—parliamentary government, democratic parties, and, the one to which my own research was initially devoted, a successful liberal movement. The Sonderweg idea was never without its critics and over time it has lost much of its hold on German historians' scholarly imagination, but it lingers on, largely because no one has come up with an equally compelling substitute.

Although the Sonderweg inspired a lot of social history, it was essentially a political concept that assumed as its basic unit of analysis the German nation state created between 1866 and 1871 and then destroyed by the Second World War. Like this Germany, the Sonderweg was also dominated by the Prussian experience which many scholars regarded as being especially responsible for the path to catastrophe. German history before 1866, therefore, was usually regarded as a kind of pre-history to the German nation state, which was assumed to be the inevitable, normative answer to the question of German identity. By the late 1970s, about the time I decided to leave Northwestern to return to Stanford, I began to wonder if this was the only way, or even the best way to think about German history. The immediate impetus for this was that I had agreed to write a volume on Germany for the Oxford History of Modern Europe; my volume was supposed to cover the period before 1866, that is, before national unification, and was designed to precede Gordon Craig's extraordinarily successful account of the years between 1866 and 1945. I quickly realized that the central question posed by my project was the nature of the subject itself: Craig's book was about the life and death of a German nation state, that is, about Bismarck's and Hitler's Germany from its beginning in the Austro-Prussian War to its terrible end in 1945. This was, to be sure, an important way of thinking about German history—no sensible person could deny the significance of the German nation state. But if one stepped back and looked at the German past—and the German present—in a broader perspective, then the Germany of 1866 to 1945 seemed like just one of many Germanies, some larger (including Austria and Switzerland), some smaller (including the regional variety that had always characterized

German Europe). The Germany created in 1866 was surely not an accident, but it was also not inevitable and not the only possible outcome to what I came to see as a complex, open-ended historical process. I tried to make these arguments in an essay entitled "What is German history?" that was meant to serve as a kind of prologue to my book for the Oxford series.

Although I did not make it explicit in this essay, there was a political dimension to what might seem like a purely historiographical argument. And that had to do with how one thought about the two German states that had emerged from the wreckage of Hitler's Third Reich. Now I had no illusions about the character of East Germany, the German Democratic Republic, the rather shabby and mean-spirited—if rarely murderous—regime that had been imposed by the Red Army on the Russian occupation zone. But like many others who were uncomfortable with Cold War orthodoxies, I believed that the best way to make life better for the people living in East Germany was to accept the legitimacy of the regime, normalize relations with it, and hope for the best. This meant accepting the demise of Bismarck's Germany and abandoning—or at least indefinitely postponing—the goal of recreating it, which remained the official policy of the Federal Republic and its western allies. In this sense, my modest scholarly efforts to rethink the German past were shaped by the political climate of the 1970s in which political initiatives like Willy Brandt's Ostpolitik were trying to open new possibilities for the German future.

After finishing my book on German history from 1770 to 1866, I went to Berlin to begin a sabbatical at the Wissenschaftskolleg. The month was October, the year 1989.

I wish I could tell you that three decades of teaching and writing about German history had enabled me to predict the outcome of the crisis that had then begun to unfold throughout Eastern Europe in the fall of 1989. Unfortunately there exists in the family archives a letter that I wrote to my wife during the afternoon of November 9 in which I confidently predicted that the Berlin Wall would not last another year—in a sense, I suppose you could say that my prediction was accurate, even if it was off by some 364 days and several hours. I can take some consolation from the fact that I was by no means the only person surprised by the fall of the wall that evening—a German political scientist recently called November 9 "the Black Friday of the Social Sciences."

Although decades of studying German history did not help me predict the fall of the wall, they did enormously enrich my experiences in Berlin during the months thereafter. I vividly remember walking around the Reichstag just after the wall had opened and remembering how many things had happened on this date, within a few blocks of where I stood: the proclamation of the first German republic in 1918 and, twenty years later, the outbreak of anti-Semitic violence called Kristallnacht, an important milestone on the road to the Holocaust. Never before had I so strongly felt the force of those two senses of living in history.

Throughout the rest of 1989 and the first half of 1990, I had a front row seat on the dramatic events that would eventually lead to the end of the GDR and the creation of a new Germany. I spent a great deal of time that year talking to people from the east, professors from the university, former government officials, and a variety of writers, translators, and others. While I had been surprised by the events of November 9, I was not surprised by the fact that, without the wall, the East German regime would not survive. It seemed to me that once people were free to leave the east, the choice was between unifying the two German states or watching a continuation of the massive movement of the population from east to west, what someone called "German unification on west German soil." In my mind, the question was not if, but how unification would occur—especially if it could be done in a peaceful and orderly manner. Among the people I spent time with in late 1989 and early 1990 were men and women who had been committed to the East German regime—even if some of them had also been critical of it. They were reluctant to accept the fact that it would not survive: watching their gradual recognition that the world—their world—was collapsing around them was an extraordinarily moving and instructive experience.

A year later, in the spring of 1991, I accompanied my wife who was giving a series of lectures in various locations in western Germany. While we were there, everyone we knew was debating the question of whether the new Germany's capital should stay in Bonn (which most of our friends favored) or move to Berlin (which I myself thought was an essential step towards unifying east and west, as well as a necessary acknowledgment of Germans' national identity). For someone who had spent years studying the German question, the Hauptstadt debate brought past and present together in an especially powerful way: everywhere we went, people were debating not simply their future, but their relationship to the past. There were, I must admit, moments when I thought to myself, "They're doing all this for me."

In retrospect, I now realize that this intense engagement with Germany's past, present, and future between 1989 and 1991 marked a turning point in my scholarly interests. After 1991, the German question began to seem less urgent that it had once been, and while I continued to write about German issues, I was more and more drawn to European, even global problems. The international system, which had seemed so stagnant during the final stages of the Cold War, was full of new opportunities and dangers. In both my teaching and research, this new sense of movement suggested new questions. It was, once again, an example of how the present points us towards different aspects of the past, how living in history shapes the kind of history we need to know. That I only became fully aware of this change in emphasis as I sat down to write these remarks illustrates Kierkegaard's well-known remark that while we can only understand our life backwards, we must live it forwards.

Part I

2

What Is German History? Reflections on the Role of the Nation in German History and Historiography
*

The question of boundaries is the first to be encountered; from it all others flow. To draw a boundary around anything is to define, analyse, and reconstruct it, in this case select, indeed adopt, a philosophy of history.

F. Braudel[1]

At the end of the sixteenth century, when the humanist and geographer Matthias Quad tried to find the boundaries for "Germany," he was forced to conclude that "there is no country in all of Christendom which embraces so many lands under one name." Two hundred years later, Goethe and Schiller wrote their famous epigram: "Germany? But where is it? I don't know how to find such a country." In 1832, Leopold

---

*Originally published in the *Journal of Modern History*, 53, no. 1 (March 1981), pp. 1–23. John Boyer, Otto Büsch, Gordon Craig, Leonard Hochberg, and James Roberts all made helpful suggestions about how to improve this essay. Of course none of them is responsible for the opinions expressed here or for the errors which remain.
[1] F. Braudel, *The Mediterranean and the Mediterranean World in the Age of Philip II* (New York, 1972), vol. I, p. 18.

von Ranke remained pessimistic that an answer to this question might easily be found:

> Who will be able to grasp in a word or concept what is German? Who will call it by name, the genius of our country, of the past and of the future? It would only be another phantom to lure us on one more false road.

By the time Ranke expressed these doubts, the search for German identity had become a burning political issue, which led many of his contemporaries to try to define their country, linguistically, geographically, or historically.[2] No wonder that from his French exile, Heinrich Heine found the whole question faintly ridiculous:

> Where does the German begin? Where does it end? May a German smoke? The majority says no. May a German wear gloves? Yes, but only of buffalo hide. . . . But a German may drink beer, indeed as a true son of Germania he should drink beer.[3]

These centuries of uncertainty about national identity provide the backdrop against which the impact of the Reichsgründung must be seen and its significance measured. It seemed, to some Germans at least, that in 1871 the question of German identity had finally been settled. When Heinrich von Treitschke published the first volume of his German History in 1879, he knew what Germany was. The victorious wars of unification

---

[2] Quad is quoted in Gerald Strauss, *Sixteenth–Century Germany: Its Topography and Topographers* (Madison, Wisconsin, 1959), pp. 40–41; Goethe and Schiller's epigram is from *Die Xenien aus Schiller's Musenalmanach für das Jahr 1797* (Danzig, 1833), p. 109; Ranke, *Über die Trennung und die Einheit von Deutschland, Sämmtliche Werke* (Leipzig, 1887), vol. 49/50, p. 172. For a concise summary of the changing meanings of the nation in German history, see W. Conze, *Die Deutsche Nation* (Göttingen, 1963).

[3] Heinrich Heine, "Über Ludwig Börne" (1840), *Werke*, ed. M. Greiner (Berlin and Cologne, 1962), 2, pp. 752–53.

had fixed its boundaries at last, for the future and also for the past. Germany was Bismarck's Reich; and German history was the story of how this Reich came to be, a story to be told over and over again so that Germans might come to feel a "delight in their fatherland" and thereby reaffirm its legitimacy as the answer to the German question.[4]

Treitschke's masterpiece helped to consolidate a remarkably powerful and persistent historiographical tradition. To the members of his scholarly generation and of those immediately following, the formation of the Reich was the central historical event. Treitschke and successors told its story very well; they filled it with heroes and villains, determination and distractions, opportunities missed and victories ultimately won. But they never forgot that the main lines of the story were set, first by the existence of the German Volk as a natural, cultural entity and second, by the destiny of the Prussian state to give this Volk its necessary political expression. Over the years, the determinist and Prussocentric emphasis of this historiographical tradition weakened somewhat. Treitschke's strident advocacy of his cause gave way to more subtle and differentiated presentations of the national pageant. Few modern German historians, however, doubted that the problem of nation building was their central theme and even fewer questioned the role of nation as the basic conceptual unit within which historical problems were to be defined.[5]

---

[4] Gordon Craig has edited a convenient selection of Treitschke's work and provided a fine introduction: *History of Germany in the Nineteenth Century* (Chicago and London, 1975). See especially pp. xiii–xiv.

[5] There is, of course, an immense literature on the *kleindeutsch* school. G. P. Gooch's *History and Historians in the Nineteenth Century* (Boston, 1959) remains the best introduction. A sharper and more analytical treatment can be found in Georg Iggers, *The German Conception of History* (Middletown, Conn., 1968).

There was, of course, nothing uniquely German about this phenomenon. In every country the dominant historiographical tradition reflects the political forces which define the boundaries of the nation. We need only think of how often the history of the United States (and frequently of its northeastern provinces) is presented as "American history" or of how often the history of England becomes "British history" in order to find examples closer to home.[6] Nor is the preeminence of the nation as a historical problem and historiographical category peculiar to Treitschke and his heirs. Everywhere in nineteenth-century Europe, the political triumph of the nation over the life of the present helped to ensure its conceptual triumph over the study of the past. As the readers of this journal well know, most modern history is national history.

What may be somewhat remarkable about the German situation is the way in which the historiographical preeminence of the nation persists even after the historical existence of the nation has been disrupted. In both of the successor states to the Reich, German historians have continued to accept the kleindeutsch definition of their nation, even while they were attacking the other ideological and methodological premises of Treitschke and his followers. The major issues in recent German historiography-the economic foundations of the Reich, the nature of German imperialism, the origins of the world wars, the failure of democracy, and the rise of Nazism-have almost all been seen as national problems, best confronted within the boundaries of the Bismarckian state. Although German historians these days seem to disagree about almost everything, the one thing most of them still accept is the historiographical legitimacy of the settlement of 1871. In this sense, the old Kaiserreich lingers on, some three decades

---

[6] See John Pocock's intelligent treatment of this issue in "British History: A Plea for a New Subject," *Journal of Modern History,* 47 (December 1975): pp. 601ff, especially pp. 611–14.

after its historical demise, as an afterimage on the national retina.[7]

Now it is not my intention in this essay to deny either the importance of Bismarck's Germany or that of the historical process from which it emerged. I do want to insist, however, that the Kaiserreich is not the only, natural, and inevitable answer to the question, What is German history? We have, I think, too often allowed the political sovereignty of the nation state to become the basis for the conceptual sovereignty of the nation as a way of thinking about the past. Political sovereignty enforces clear boundaries, imposes separations, and insists on the primacy of national forms. But human affairs are often not so neat and easy to package. Our histories come in many different shapes. It may be time to give up the idea that all of those living in a nation possess only one past and to accept the fact that nations, like every other sort of complex group, contain many different histories which often converge, overlap, or intersect, but which sometimes move in quite different directions. Surely we must be alert to the connections among these histories, but that does not mean that we must force them into a single mold. If we recognize this multiplicity, we lose what I take to be an often illusory cohesion; we gain a

---

[7] Here are three discussions of postwar historiography, each one reflecting a particular phase in the development of the period since 1945: Hans Rothfels, "Zur Krise des Nationalstaats," *Vierteljahrshefte für Zeitgeschichte*, 1, no. 2 (1953): pp. 138–52; Ernst Nolte, "Zur Konzeption der Nationalgeschichte heute," *Historische Zeitschrift*, 202, no. 3 (1966): pp. 603–21; and Werner Conze, "Das Kaiserreich von 1871 als gegenwärtige Vergangenheit im Generationswechsel der deutschen Geschichtsschreibung," *Staat und Gesellschaft im politischen Wandel* (Bussmann Festschrift), ed. W. Pols (Stuttgart, 1979), pp. 383–405. Hans-Ulrich Wehler's essay, "Geschichtswissenschaft heute," *Stichworte zur geistigen Situation der Zeit, Vol. 2: Politik und Kultur*, (Stuttgart, 1979), pp. 709–53, provides a survey of postwar German historiography from a rather different perspective.

richer view of the past and a much sharper sense of the historical questions which lie ahead of us.[8]

Traditionally, the story of the German past has been used as a case study for the process of nation building. Understandably so: the creation of a united Germany dominated European history in the second half of the nineteenth century, just as its destruction dominated European history in the first half of the twentieth. And yet, if we shift the picture of the German past just slightly, its pieces fall together in a different way. The purpose of this essay is to argue that in addition to being a model for nation building, German history also provides a case study of the nation's limitations, both as a historical force and as historiographical category. Once we stop assuming that Germany must mean Bismarck's Germany, we can see that German history is made up of a more complex and a much richer set of political, social, economic, and cultural developments, which are sometimes national in scope, but which often exist within, or extend beyond, national boundaries.[9]

Let us begin by adopting a resolutely nominalist stance with regard to the question of German identity in the eighteenth

---

[8] For a sophisticated account of how the concept of "history" became associated with a singular process, see R. Koselleck's article on "Geschichte" in *Geschichtliche Grundbegriffe*, ed. Otto Brunner et al. (Stuttgart, 1975), 2, p. 653. The way in which different "histories" can coexist even within a small community is illustrated in B. Cohn's stimulating essay "The Pasts of an Indian Village," *Comparative Studies in Society and History*, 3 (1961): pp. 241–49.

[9] Peter Katzenstein's *Disjoined Partners: Austria and Germany since 1815* (Berkeley and Los Angeles, 1976) is a stimulating attempt to view the history of central Europe as an example of failed national cohesion rather than one of triumph. Katzenstein tries to explain why Germany and Austria did not unite, despite the powerful ties of their shared language, etc. Historians may find the book overly schematic, but they will certainly benefit from the originality of the questions and the data Katzenstein assembles to answer them.

century. That means we cannot accept the conventional ways of avoiding the issue. We cannot, for instance, identify Germany with one of its parts, such as Prussia; nor can we impose the kleindeutsch Reich anachronistically, pretending that the Germany of 1771 was the Germany of 1871 in utero; nor can we simply assume that there must be something called "Germany," a particular territory, a set of ideas and institutions, or a cluster of traits and customs. It is, of course, this last assumption that we must seek to test. If we look at the history of central Europe in the eighteenth century, can we find German experiences which were both common and distinctive—experiences, in other words, which Germans shared with one another but not with anybody else?

Some answers to this question can be excluded without difficulty. German history in the eighteenth century is definitely not the history of those inhabiting a clearly defined part of Europe. Even a cursory look at the map reveals the rich variety of landscapes in which Germans lived, the abundance of barriers separating them from one another, and the absence of natural frontiers separating them from their neighbors. Our consideration of the physical map prepares us for what we find when we begin to draw cultural and linguistic boundaries. Within the German lands, there was a rich variety of dialects and cultural distinctions. Between Germans and other language groups, it is very hard to draw sharp lines. Border regions are often wide belts of mixed settlement; and even when divisions can be established, islands of linguistic minorities exist on either side of them. There was, in short, no terrain, no place, no region which we can call "Germany." This fact distinguished the geographical basis of modern German history from that of countries such as Britain, Spain, or Italy. All of these countries had (and still have) profoundly difficult problems of national cohesion, but all of them, unlike "Germany," have a fairly well-defined area within which these problems can be confronted. Germany, to alter Metternich's famous line about Italy, may have sometimes been more than a "geographical expression," but it was always something less.[10]

Eighteenth-century political boundaries are no less elusive than physical and linguistic ones. Central Europe's political fragmentation in the early modern period is well known. Small states, free cities, ecclesiastical territories, and semi-autonomous estates were scattered across the political landscape in bewildering profusion. And even this array of political units is a good deal less cohesive than it might seem if we think of political sovereignty in our own terms. Many of these "states" were themselves cut up by a number of internal civil, judicial, and fiscal boundaries; some were not made up of contiguous pieces, but were joined only by the ruler's personal sovereignty; others had to endure enclaves of independence or conflicting sovereignty within their borders. Looked at from a broad perspective, therefore, "German politics" appears as a hopelessly complicated web of conflicting jurisdictions, uncertain sovereignties, and deep local divisions. Looked at from the perspective of most contemporaries, on the other hand, there was no such thing as a "German politics." Like most other Europeans, an individual's political world was a small and personal one, limited to the village, town, or estate in which he lived.[11]

Hovering over most, but not all, of these political units was the Holy Roman Empire, the entity a majority of contemporaries would have had in mind if they had used the term Deutschland in a political sense. Even if we are willing to

[10] Introductions to the problems of German geography can be found in the following general works: R. E. Dickinson, *Germany: A General and Regional Geography* (London and New York, 1961); E. deMartonne, *Europe central,* 2 vols. (Paris, 1930–31); A. Mutton, *Central Europe: A Regional Human Geography,* 2nd ed. (London, 1968).
[11] On these issues, see D. Gerhard, "Regionalismus und ständisches Wesen als ein Grundthema europäischer Geschichte," *Historische Zeitschrift,* 174, no. 2 (1952), pp. 307–38.

overlook the fact that the empire included some non-Germans
and excluded many Germans, we can accept it as an answer to
the question of German identity only with some important
reservations. First, by the eighteenth century the empire did
not mean much in some areas, especially in the two most
important states in central Europe, Prussia and Austria.
Second, even where the empire did have a political role to play,
this role involved guaranteeing diversity rather than imposing
cohesion. The empire worked best where it unified least, which
is why it was most popular among those who benefited from
political fragmentation and thus sought protection from their
larger neighbors. The history of the empire is a kind of German
history, therefore, but it is a history which shows us political
variety in a new and vivid fashion. As one recent student of the
old Reich has put it, "German history [in the early modern
period] must be recognized for what it is, a vigorous
entanglement of component parts."[12]

Political fragmentation reflected, and was in turn reinforced
by, economic conditions in eighteenth-century central Europe.
The communications network was poor. Roads were almost
always primitive, hard to use at best, impassable when the
weather was bad. River traffic was impeded by natural hazards
and by a frustrating profusion of tolls and restrictions.
Economic activity, therefore, tended to be locked in separate

---

[12] G. Benecke, *Society and Politics in Germany, 1500–1750* (London and
Toronto, 1974), p. 161. The historiography of the Holy Roman
Empire is an interesting example of how the use of national
categories can distort our vision. For generations, historians of
eighteenth-century Germany emphasized the failures and
weaknesses of the Empire. Only recently have we begun to realize
that to accuse the Empire of failing as a nation state is to criticize it
for losing a game it never intended to play. Gerald Strauss has given
us a useful introduction to the new scholarly view of the Empire in
his review essay, "The Holy Roman Empire Revisited," *Central
European History*, 2, no. 3 (1978): pp. 290–301.

islands, which were then linked by intermediaries to a regional system of markets. Quite distinct from these local economies were the rather small number of enterprises which engaged in commerce across national and linguistic frontiers. These firms, usually to be found only in commercial centers such as Frankfurt and Hamburg, were part of an international system of exchange. For our purposes, it is important to emphasize that there was nothing particularly German about either the local or the international economies. Farmers and craftsmen had little contact with their counterparts in other regions, and none of them had much in common with the bankers and merchants who moved upon a European stage. There was no common currency or legislation, no communications network or national market center which joined all of them together. And so, when their various goods moved from place to place, they were taxed like any others. To the tax official or toll collector, there were no "German goods"; everything beyond the boundaries of their own localities was equally foreign.[13]

At the beginning of the eighteenth century, central European cultures, like central European economies, were either locally confined or internationally extended.[14] Most Germans lived in a cultural world which was no larger than their social or economic sphere. These worlds formed islands of local customs and relationships, festivity and folklore, which were set apart from the rest of society by dialect and tradition,

---

[13] Jan DeVries has an excellent analysis of the problems of early modern economies in *The Economy of Europe in an Age of Crisis, 1600–1750* (Cambridge, 1976). For the German situation, the best place to begin is Hermann Aubin and Wolfgang Zorn, eds., *Handbuch der deutschen Wirtschafts—und Sozialgeschichte*, vol. I (Stuttgart, 1971).

[14] I am using *culture* here to mean a set of shared symbols and values. It is important to note that this definition assumes that culture is a process, not just a body of ideas and artifacts; it is shared symbols, not just symbols. One must always be aware, therefore, of the institutional network through which the sharing takes place.

as well as by the limitations on scale which oral communication inevitably imposes. A few Germans belonged to cultural systems which stretched across frontiers; like the non-local economies of the eighteenth century, these cultures usually had a European base. Such cultures included the small realms of the aristocracy, the upper ranks of the church, and certain sectors of academic life. Their range was restricted, not by dialect and orality, but by ascriptive status or by the need to acquire unusual skills. Once again it is important to note that there is not much we can call German in either the local cultures of the masses or the European cultures of the elites.[15]

The first attempt to create a German culture had been part of the Protestant revolt against the corruption of the Roman church. Luther's translation of the Bible, perhaps the most important cultural product of this movement, helped to lay the foundation for a German literary language and public. But the ability of this foundation to expand was limited, first by its links to the powerful religious conflicts which divided Germans, and second, by the narrowness of its intellectual range. In the late seventeenth and early eighteenth centuries, a secular German culture began to build upon, but also to extend these religious foundations. This was essentially a literary culture, composed of readers and writers who were joined through an expanding network of publishers, periodicals, lending libraries, and reading societies. This literary culture seemed open and unrestricted, a fact its participants underscored when they spoke of themselves as a public and when they urged that the sphere of publicity, the Öffentlichkeit, should be free. In fact, eighteenth-century literary culture was able to extend across territorial and social barriers. Threads made up of printed

---

[15] The condition of the German theater illustrates this point: at the beginning of the eighteenth century, theatrical presentations were either part of local festivities or foreign productions given at courts. See W. A. Bruford, *Theatre, Drama, and Audience in Goethe's Germany* (London, 1950).

pages and personal connections linked people from Strassburg to Riga, from Hamburg to Vienna. Most of those involved were fairly well-off members of the educated and propertied sectors of society, but some ambitious members of the lower orders also participated, often at great personal cost. To them, literary skills and accomplishments seemed to offer an escape, either vicarious or physical, from the confines of their local worlds. In comparison to the various elite or popular cultures, therefore, the new public had within it the potential to engage everyone who knew German. It was, its spokesmen hoped, the basis for a national community, a Volk.[16]

Eighteenth-century literary culture was the beginning of what we now usually think of as German culture, the culture of Goethe, Schiller, and their great contemporaries. We must bear in mind, however, that this culture only touched a small minority of central Europeans in the eighteenth century. It was a national culture in aspiration, but never, and certainly not before 1800, in actuality. Literature, literacy, even language may make the formation of a national culture. They are possible causes, not sufficient ones. In cultural life, as in the realm of politics and economics, there is no single connected pattern which we can regard as German. There are instead many patterns, many different sorts of experiences and institutions, symbols and relationships, which sometimes touch or even coincide, but which often remain quite separate.[17]

---

[16] For a guide to the recent work on the social history of eighteenth-century literature, see Gerhard Sauder, "Sozialgeschichtliche Aspekte der Literatur im 18. Jahrhundert," *Internationales Archiv für Sozialgeschichte der deutschen Literatur*, 4 (1979): pp. 197–241. The older literature is surveyed in Eva Becker and Manfred Dehn, eds., *Literarisches Leben* (Hamburg, 1968).

[17] David Potter has a characteristically acute and insightful comment on the problem of assuming that the existence of common language, literature, and the like explains the formation of a nation or nationality. This assumption, he points out, "tends to conceal the

Edward Fox has suggested a way of making sense out of these patterns. Fox's work is based on his study of France, but it seems no less relevant to German history. There were, Fox argues, essentially two sorts of institutions in traditional French society. The first he calls areal, by which he means the relationships among those living within contained territorial units. These units would usually be quite small, limited to the distance someone might walk in a day, within the walls of a city, a primary market region, a handful of villages. As we have seen, for the overwhelming majority of central Europeans in the eighteenth century, political, economic, and cultural activities were areal. Fox calls the second pattern of institutions linear. These institutions are based upon relationships among people who do not necessarily live near to one another, but who do share some social position, commercial interest, or cultural proclivity which links them across space. The economic ties among merchants and bankers were linear, as were the social bonds connecting the aristocracy and the cultural connections among members of the reading public.[18]

There are, of course, areal and linear institutions in almost all social systems larger than a tribe. The point to be stressed about eighteenth-century central Europe is that these were the only two sorts available. It is also worth emphasizing how our inclination to think in national terms makes it difficult for us

---

fact that the formation of a nation or of a nationality is a process of the creation of conditions of commonality, and that as a process it cannot be explained by taking a fixed set of ingredients and saying that when these ingredients or most of them are put in a one end of the machine, a nation will come out the other." "Historians and the Problem of Large-Scale Community Formation," in *History and American Society*, ed. David Potter (New York, 1973), pp. 55–56.

[18] Edward Whiting Fox, *History in Geographic Perspective: The Other France* (New York, 1971), especially pp. 37–39 and 56. I am grateful to Len Hochburg for calling Fox's work to my attention and showing me its relevance to the problems addressed in this essay.

to take this point fully into account. National categories tend to make us look for large territorial units and thus to undervalue institutions with smaller scale and local scope. At the same time, national categories encourage us to assume that institutions are integrated and congruent and that they have a clearly defined territorial location—in other words, to think that institutions are always as they seem to be in a modern nation. But this assumption can lead us to overlook those linear ties which had no territorial base or spatial existence, but which did join people together in practically and symbolically powerful ways.

What then is German history in the eighteenth century? It is the history of these areal and linear institutions which gave shape and meaning to people's lives. It is the history of cultural richness and political diversity, of social fragmentation and economic isolation. It is also the history of the first faint stirrings toward national cohesion, the initial movement toward the creation of a German culture and society. But in writing the history of this movement, we must not confuse aspirations with accomplishments by positing the existence of some fictional entity we can call Germany. To do so obscures what may be the central fact about the era: German history, as a singular process, had not yet really begun.

The limitations imposed on our vision by national categories are every bit as troublesome for an understanding of the nineteenth century as they were for our understanding of the eighteenth. In fact, as we watch the historical process of national unification pick up momentum, it becomes harder and harder for us to see those aspects of the German experience which do not fit neatly into the story of the Reichsgründung. A glance at any bibliography of nineteenth-century German history will demonstrate the effect this has had on the scholarly literature. The closer ideas, events, or individuals are to the emergence of the kleindeutsch Reich, the more they have been studied. Problems in the history of German economics, culture, and politics which seem to be outside of the nation building process are frequently ignored or pushed to the periphery of the established view. Of course there is a great deal of German local and regional history, most of it to be found in the historical publications of various states and cities. Characteristically, this is history written and read by those in the locality itself; it is of interest only to people who share the experiences of the Heimat. It is difficult, therefore, to think of works on regional history which have had a major impact on German national historiography, comparable to Vann Woodward's book on the American south or Georges Lefebvre's on the Nord. Along these lines it is worth noting that Johannes Ziekursch is best known to most students of German history for his workmanlike study of the Kaiserreich; his much more interesting and innovative works on Silesian social history are infrequently cited and difficult to find.[19]

Another illustration of this point is what Frank B. Tipton has called the "national consensus" in the study of German economic history. This consensus is based upon the subordination of economic history to political developments; more specifically, it involves fusing problems of economic growth with problems of national unification. The national consensus has had implications for the way German economic historians define their subject, for the sorts of questions they ask, and for the evidence they use to get their answers. Most often, they have studied economic life in state or national units, have emphasized the importance of political institutions and state policy as a factor in economic development, and have used administrative records as the most important source of their evidence.[20]

---

[19] On Ziekursch, see the article by Karl-Georg Faber, in Hans-Ulrich Wehler, ed., *Deutsche Historiker*, vol 3 (Göttingen,1972), pp. 109–23.
[20] Frank B. Tipton, "The National Consensus in German Economic History," *Central European History*, 7, no. 3 (1974): pp. 195–224. See also the very interesting analysis in Richard Tilly, "Los von England:

Consider, for instance, the conventional view of the Zollverein, the Customs Union established by Prussia and a number of other German states in the 1830s. W. O. Henderson, the author of the classic work on this subject, had no doubts about the purpose of his research: "My account endeavored to show that the establishment of the Customs Union—and other economic developments—helped to prepare the way for the subsequent unification of Germany."[21] Henderson, like the majority of scholars who have worked on the Zollverein, simply assumed that it had an important economic impact. His major concern was with the bureaucratic decisions which led to its formation and extension. Furthermore, once the union was in place, it became the basis for talking about a German economy, which was historically linked to the national economic system established in 1866–1871. One does not have to question the value of Henderson's work in order to point out that it has some very significant limitations. In the first place, it leaves unanswered, because it leaves unasked, the question of whether the Customs Union did in fact encourage economic growth. According to Tipton, this proposition cannot be demonstrated with the existing data. Second, Henderson's analysis of governmental economic policy does not tell us very much about economic behavior, in large part because data on what administrators think is happening or on what they want to have happen are often not very good indicators of what individual enterprises are in fact doing. Finally, and for our present purposes most importantly, it is misleading to talk about a German economy in the 1830s, when local, regional, and transnational economic relationships

---

Probleme des Nationalismus in der deutschen Wirtschaftsgeschichte," *Zeitschrift für die gesamte Staatswissenschaft*, 124, no. 1 (1968): pp. 179–96.

[21] W. O. Henderson, *The Zollverein*, 2nd ed, (Chicago, 1959), pp. v–vi.

almost certainly remained of much greater importance for most central Europeans.[22]

Some of the same limitations that exist in the traditional historiography of the Zollverein can be found in the historical literature on the economic aspects of the Reichsgründung. Even the title of Eugen Franz's pioneering work on this subject, *Der Entscheidungskampf um die wirtschaftspolitische Führung Deutschlands (1856-1867)*, suggests his main purpose, which was to show how "farsighted statesmen made the German economy into a foundation for the new Reich."[23] In fact, Franz studied the statesmen, but not the economy. Like Henderson, he assumed that there must be a direct link between state policy and economic behavior and also that developments which encouraged the political integration of Germany must have encouraged German economic growth. Neither of these assumptions is self-evidently true. When Helmut Boehme studied this same cluster of issues three decades later, he gave his analysis a very different ideological edge, but, like Franz, he concentrated on state policy, political controversies, and the problems of nation building. Boehme's main contributions, therefore, were to the scholarly debate about the political and social origins and implications of the Reichsgründung. As

---

[22] Tipton, "National Consensus," p. 202. For other efforts to reassess the meaning of the Zollverein, see Tilly's article cited in note 20; Helmut Berding, "Die Entstehung des deutschen Zollvereins als Problem historischer Forschung," in *Vom Staat des Ancien Regime zum modernen Parteienstaat. Festschrift für Theodor Schieder*, ed. Helmut Berding (Munich and Vienna, 1978), pp. 225–37; and Rolf Horst Dumke, "Intra-German Trade in 1837 and Regional Economic Development," *Vierteljahrsschrift für Sozial– und Wirtschaftsgeschichte*, 64, no. 4 (1977): pp. 468–96. Sidney Pollard questions the usefulness of national categories in his important essay on "Industrialization and the European Economy," *Economic History Review*, 2nd Series, 26, no. 4 (1973): pp. 636–48.

[23] Eugen Franz, *Der Kampf um die wirtschaftspolitische Führung Deutschlands (1856–1867)* (Munich, 1933), p. 436.

Richard Tilly pointed out in his thoughtful assessment of German economic history, "For all its concern with industrialization, [Boehme's book] is basically addressed to conventional historians interested in Bismarckian Machtpolitik."[24]

There is no doubt about the fact that Henderson, Franz, and Böhme have helped us to see the economic dimensions of nation- building. But they have not told us very much about economic development. Nor have they clarified the role of economic behavior-as opposed to economic policy-in preparing the way for an integrated political system. In order to perform this very important task we must not only use different sorts of evidence, we must also be willing to suspend our belief in the necessary primacy of national units. In other words, to see if markets, institutional relationships, and entrepreneurial decisions actually were moving toward a national system after 1850, it is not enough to show that there was a significant growth in economic relationships within the Zollverein. There was, after all, an absolute growth throughout the economy during this period. What must be demonstrated is that "national" economic activity was relatively more important than regional and international activity. This can only be done by studying these various levels together. Otherwise one obscures precisely those questions one should be trying to answer.[25]

---

[24] Helmut Böhme, *Deutschlands Weg zur Grossmacht. Studien zum Verhältnis von Wirtschaft und Staat während der Reichsgründungszeit, 1848–81* (Berlin, 1966). Richard Tilly, "Soll und Haben: Recent German Economic History and the Problem of Economic Development," *Journal of Economic History*, 29, no. 2 (June 1969): p. 310.

[25] This sort of objection can, I think, be raised against Wolfgang Zorn's work on national economic integration, the most recent example of which is his article, "Zwischenstaatliche wirtschaftliche Integration im Deutschen Zollverein, 1867–1870," *Vierteljahrsschrift für Sozial—und Wirtschaftsgeschichte*, 65, no. 1 (1978): pp. 38–76. On

"German culture," like the "German economy," is an abstraction which encourages us to focus our attention on one sort of historical experience at the expense of others. To most historians, nineteenth-century German culture is an extension of that literary culture which I mentioned a moment ago, the culture of scholarship and "serious" literature, of the universities and the major national periodicals, of established artists and musicians. Our libraries are filled with the products of this culture and with more than a century of criticism and historical analysis based upon them. But if we look for a moment at the data measuring the distribution of national periodicals or at the number of people who attended universities or at the cost of books, we recognize that this national culture touched no more than a minority. To most craftsmen and farmers, to villagers and the urban poor, to domestic servants and common soldiers-in short, to the over-whelming majority of the population-national literary culture meant very little. These people had no access to the long, tightly printed columns of the Nationalzeitung; they had no interest in the scholarly articles published in the Staatslexikon; they could not afford the time or the money to read the latest work by Freytag or Raabe. This culture was not their culture.[26]

---

the growth of economic relationships on every level, but especially internationally, see Sidney Pollard, *European Economic Integration, 1815–1970* (London, 1974).

[26] Pioneering work on this subject has been done by Rudolf Schenda; see especially his *Volk ohne Buch: Studien zur Sozialgeschichte der populären Lesestoffe, 1770–1910* (Frankfurt, 1970). Also of great interest are the essays by Rolf Engelsing, for example, *Analphabetentum und Lektüre. Zur Sozialgeschichte des Lesens in Deutschland* (Stuttgart, 1973). There are valuable data on this issue in Ilsedore Rarisch, *Industrialisierung und Literatur. Buchproduktion, Verlagswesen und Buchhandel in Deutschland im 19. Jahrhundert in ihrem statistischen Zusammenhang* (Berlin, 1976).

But it would be wrong to assume, as did so many of their
contemporaries in the literary culture, that because the masses
did not belong to this culture, they had no culture of their own.
Of course, they did; of course they had a set of shared symbols
and rituals which ornamented and gave meaning to their lives.
In villages and urban neighborhoods, within particular crafts
or occupations, there were patterns of festivity, stories told and
songs sung, pious habits and traditional beliefs. Our libraries
are also filled with information about these things, but it is
stored in sections on anthropology or folklore, far away from
what we customarily regard as "culture" or "intellectual
history." It is in these remote classifications that we must look
if we are to find evidence about the cultures of most central
Europeans during the first two-thirds of the nineteenth
century.[27]

The study of popular cultures not only rescues an important
heritage from condescension and neglect, it also provides a
context within which literary culture itself must be understood.
Just as our view ·of economic integration is incomplete until
we put national patterns together with regional and
international ones, so our picture of literary culture will remain
incomplete until we uncover the complex interaction between

---

[27] The best introduction to folklore in Germany is G. Wiegelmann
et al., *Volkskunde: Eine Einführung* (Berlin, 1977). Also of value is a
special issue on Germany of the *Journal of the Folklore Institute*, 5, no.
2 (1968); and Martin Scharfe, "Towards a Cultural History: Notes on
Contemporary Volkskunde (Folklore) in German-Speaking
Countries," *Social History*, 4, no. 2 (1979): pp. 333–44. A new concern
among literary scholars for popular culture can be seen in the
recently established *Internationales Archiv für Sozialgeschichte der deutschen
Literatur* (1976–). For our purposes, the article by Günther Fetzer
and Jörg Schönert on Trivialliteratur, 2 (1977): pp. 1–39) is of special
interest. Of course the whole concept of Trivialliteratur is an
illustration of the conventional attitudes toward culture which I am
trying to question.

it and a variety of regional and social cultural systems. Did national culture gradually expand, as educational institutions and increasing literacy penetrated more and more regions and social strata? Perhaps. But isn't it equally possible that as literary culture became more complex and technical, it became less accessible to those with only rudimentary literary skills?[28]

This sort of question obviously has profound implications for the study of nineteenth-century politics. Until quite recently, however, we have been able to ignore these implications by concentrating our attention on political activity of a certain sort. "Politics" in conventional German political history was defined as the ideas and activities of those at the top, e.g., the statesmen, leaders, and ideologues who directed or wrote about state policy. In the past decade or so, historians have studied party organizations, pressure groups, and electoral behavior and we have begun to learn more about a broader range of political experiences. But even this new research on the social basis of political life is usually restricted to the politics of parliaments, parties, and pressure groups. As Mack Walker reminds us in his elegant monograph, *German Home Towns*, there were many Germans in the nineteenth century to whom this sort of politics had very little meaning.[29] In the semi-autonomous towns of the south and west which Walker studied, there was an intense public life, but one that cannot be understood with the concepts and categories designed to analyze national institutions and constitutional issues. Just as it is important not to take the lack of literary

---

[28] For a useful formulation of this question in reference to another period, see Harry Payne, "Elite versus Popular Mentality in the Eighteenth Century," *Studies in Eighteenth Century Culture*, 8 (1979): pp. 3–32. On the broader issue of elite and popular cultures, some valuable insights can be found in Peter Burke, *Popular Culture in Early Modern Europe* (New York, 1978).

[29] Mack Walker, *German Home Towns: Community, State, and General Estate, 1648–1871* (Ithaca and London, 1971).

culture to mean the lack of culture, so we must not write off as "apolitical" people who were not part of what became the national political culture.[30]

In German history, the question of when people became part of a national political culture is particularly important because it bears on the issue of popular involvement in the process of national unification.[31] Historians in the kleindeutsch tradition had a good deal of trouble confronting this issue since they sought to maintain two (not necessarily compatible) positions: first, that the formation of the Reich was part of the natural destiny of the German Volk, and second, that it was the great historic achievement of the Prussian state. They usually ended up by suggesting that the state acted as the Volk's agent, without trying to examine too closely the relationship which existed between the two. As one recent representative of this view put it, "Bismarck fulfilled the will of the Volk from above."[32] In response to this extraordinary statement, we can only ask, "What Volk?" Surely not the Reich's Polish, Danish,

---

[30] Eugen Weber's formulation of this issue is worth quoting: "The question is not whether politics existed in the countryside. Every community was, in some sense, a polis. The question is whether the local, sui generis interests there thrashed out can be interpreted in the familiar terms of national politics." *Peasants into Frenchmen* (Stanford, 1976), p. 242.

[31] The most recent discussion of this and related matters is in Otto Dann, ed., *Nationalismus und sozialer Wandel* (Hamburg, 1978). There is also a great deal of useful material in the essays edited by Theodor Schieder and Ernst Deuerlein, *Reichsgründung 1870/71* (Stuttgart, 1970).

[32] Karl Bosl, "Die Verhandlungen über den Eintritt der süddeutschen Staaten in den Norddeutschen Bund und die Entstehung der Reichsverfassung," in *Reichsgründung 1870/71*, p. 151. Roy Austensen's article, "Austria and the 'Struggle for Supremacy in Germany,' 1848–1864," *Journal of Modern History*, 52, no. 2 (June 1980): pp. 195–225, criticizes the *kleindeutsch* position from a perspective quite similar to mine.

and French minorities. And what about the supporters of the Guelph monarchy, the Saxon particularists, the south Germans and Austrians? Above all, what about the millions of uninformed and uninvolved Germans who viewed without interest or understanding the news of distant battles and irrelevant debates? These people became part of Germany in 1866-1871, but they were not in any useful sense of the word part of a self-conscious national community.[33] In Robert Berdahl's sharp formulation of this point, "The Bismarckian state was not 'pre-determined'; it was 'self-determined,' not by popular sovereignty or the Volk, but by its leading statesman."[34]

When we recognize the full force of this fact, we can then see the questions about German nation building which have too often been neglected despite more than a century of intense scholarship on the Reichsgründung: To what degree was the German state able to forge a German Volk? How and why did national connections develop in social, economic, and cultural life? What other patterns persisted and why? To address these issues, we need for Germany a book like Eugen Weber's *Peasants into Frenchmen*, a book which would show us how conscription, education, and economic development

---

[33] Even a superficial look at the electoral data suggests the shallowness of popular support for the Bismarckian Reichsgründung. In the elections of 1871, for example, just over half (52%) of the eligible voters turned up at the polls. Among these voters, no more than half can be viewed as firmly committed to the new Reich; at least fifteen percent were clearly opposed, as were a substantial number of those whose allegiance is hard to read (e.g. the Conservatives, Progressives, and Zentrum). For more on this issue and a guide to the relevant literature, see Otto Büsch, "Der Beitrag der historischen Wahlforschung zur Geschichte der deutschen und europäischen Wählerbewegung," in Büsch, ed., *Wählerbewegung in der europäischen Geschichte* (Berlin, 1980), pp. 16ff.

[34] Robert Berdahl, "New Thoughts on German Nationalism," *American Historical Review*, 77, no. 1 (1972): p. 70.

pulled people from local to national institutions.[35] As things now stand, we know about the army as a political and social institution, but not about how military service affected the way men saw themselves and their society. We know about the lives and thoughts of German academics, but not about the social impact of schools. We know about economic policy and interest groups, but not about how economic growth changed patterns of human interaction. These aspects of nation building began rather than ended with the victories of 1866–1871. Knowing about these matters and others like them will help us to understand "Germany" not simply as a formal political unit, but also as a force in the lives of its inhabitants.

What is German history during the first two-thirds of the nineteenth century? It is, among other things, the history of the Reichsgründung, of the economic, cultural, and political processes which produced a nation state in central Europe. It is the history of the Zollverein and growth of Prussian economic influence, of national elites and the expansion of a national public opinion, of better communications and rising literacy, of social integration and political mobilization. But German history is also the history of those social groups and regions which opposed these things or were untouched by them. It is the history of regional ties and social separation, of popular cultures and traditional politics. Above all, German history is the history of how these various experiences interacted and coexisted and of how one is inexplicable without the others.

In 1815, on the threshold of the great age of European nation building, Joseph de Maistre wrote that "it is not difficult to unify a nation on a map, but in reality-that is quite a different thing." More recently, Eric Wolf made the same point when he warned us not to "confuse the theory of state sovereignty with the facts of political life." We should not, in other words,

---

[35] See note 30, above.

allow the appearance of cartographical cohesion or the pretension of formal sovereignty to conceal the fact that every state is filled with what Wolf calls "interstitial, supplementary, and parallel structures."[36] These are structures which, resisting being drawn into the institutional symmetry which states try to impose, form pockets of internal separation or weave lines which stretch across legal frontiers. In the case of a new nation like the German Reich, these considerations are especially important to keep in mind. Bismarck's Germany had to be built upon, and was necessarily limited by, deeply-rooted patterns of behavior and commitment. Moreover, the new Germany did not include millions of people who had long-standing ties to German cultural, social, economic, and political life, people who did not suddenly stop being part of German history just because the Prussian army won a few battles.[37]

It is perhaps understandable, but certainly unfortunate, that the defeat of Austria in 1866 resulted in her extrusion from German historiography—just as it is regrettable that the political partition of North America resulted in the scholarly separation of Canada from "American history." A good deal might be learned if these various histories were brought together again. We know, for example, that ideas, institutions, and individuals from the Habsburg lands continued to have an

---

[36] DeMaistre is quoted in Lord Acton, *Essays in the Liberal Interpretation of History*, ed. William McNeill (Chicago and London, 1967), p. 142, note 2. See also Eric Wolf, "Kinship, Friendship, and Patron-Client Relations in Complex Societies," *The Social Anthropology of Complex Societies* (New York, 1966), p. 1.

[37] Gary Cohen's *The Prague Germans, 1861–1914: The Problems of Ethnic Survival* (Princeton, 1981) shows how German national awareness was in no way limited to the kleindeutsch Reich. For another, yet more complicated example of German history outside of Germany, see John Armstrong, "Mobilized Diaspora in Tsarist Russia: The Case of the Baltic Germans," in *Soviet Nationality Policies and Practices*, ed. J. Azrael (New York, 1978), pp. 63–104.

impact on the political life of the Kaiserreich. This was most obviously and disastrously true in the case of rightwing political movements, but the same pattern can be found elsewhere as well. Surely historians should make more of the fact that Social Democracy in Germany and Austria seems to be more alike than either is like any other party in Europe. Similarly, a grossdeutsch history of liberalism and of political Catholicism, both of which began before the division of 1866, might display the evolution of these movements in a new light.[38]

The limitation of German history to the history of the Reich is even more difficult to maintain when we turn to the realm of culture. There is a certain irony to be noted here: as we have seen, literary culture was the first truly German phenomenon, the first set of values and institutions to move between the localism of the populace and the internationalism of the elites. But the same network of printed communication which enabled this culture to spread across central Europe in the eighteenth century prevented it from being integrated into the state in the nineteenth. The hopes of people like Richard Wagner that the Reich might become a center for German art and literature were not fulfilled-as Wagner himself swiftly realized. German culture, the culture of Nietzsche and

---

[38] There have been a few efforts to see German political developments in a central European context: Hans Rosenberg's *Grosse Depression und Bismarckzeit* (Berlin, 1967), for instance, includes chapters on Austria. Significantly, this aspect of the book was not picked up by most of the scholars who have been deeply influenced by Rosenberg's work.

John Boyer's forthcoming study of Christian Socialism in Austria points the way towards a reintegration of Austrian and "German" history, since Boyer's work is informed by a sensitivity to the similarities and differences between the two political cultures. Another recent work on Austrian history which emphasizes the broader central European context is Harm-Hinrich Brandt's *Der österreichische Neoabsolutismus. Staatsfinanzen und Politik, 1848–1860*, 2 vols., (Göttingen, 1978).

Burckhardt, of Freud and Kafka, of Max Frisch and Bert Brecht, was never contained within a single state.[39] Indeed, the more insistently a single state pressed its claims to be the Germany, the more fragmented and diffuse German culture became. Never in German history were its cultural resources more scattered and disconnected than they were between 1938 and 1945, the time when more Germans were part of the same political system than ever before. If we wish to put "German culture" into a historical context, therefore, we must not take its national location for granted, but rather try to trace a much wider pattern of connections, made possible by shared language and literature, and sustained by a complex web of educational institutions, scholarly associations, publishing enterprises, and personal connections.

If the nation state is too narrow to contain certain kinds of relationships, it is too broad a field to capture others. A good deal of German economic activity, for example, is not easily understood on the national level, despite the obvious importance of the central government as a source of legislation, fiscal policy, and monetary unity. One scholar has even argued that political unification may have increased the importance of regional differences by accentuating the contrast between industrial and agrarian areas within the Reich. A great many contemporaries, among them some of the most outspoken advocates of national sovereignty, were certainly aware that their regions had special interests which were quite

---

[39] The *locus classicus* for a statement on the incompatibility of the nation state and culture is of course Jacob Burckhardt's *Force and Freedom: Reflections on History* (New York, 1943), pp. 183ff. For a sensitive historical analysis, see Theodor Schieder's *Das deutsche Kaiserreich von 1871 als Nationalstaat* (Cologne and Opladen, 1961), especially pp. 55ff.

different from those of the nation as a whole.[40] In some cases, the centrifugal force of regionalism was increased by linkages between the region and non-German economic systems. And of course there were some German firms with essentially international horizons, firms which operated in world-wide markets for the movement of capital, commodities, and technological innovations. We are not in a position to evaluate the relative strength of national, local, and international economic systems. Only one thing is clear: such an evaluation will involve trying to see all of these levels of economic life together.[41]

National units are also unwieldy for the study of social groups and institutions. Indeed a concentration on national affairs, together with the political orientation such a concentration usually brings with it, has tended to block from our vision large areas of study. This may be one reason why the history of women and family life has not, at least until quite recently, received very much attention from German historians.[42] As we move into those areas of human experience

---

[40] Frank B. Tipton, *Regional Variations in the Economic Development of Germany during the Nineteenth Century* (Middletown, Conn., 1976) argues that regional economic differences increased after political unity was achieved. Knut Borchardt has a powerful analysis of one aspect of this issue in his article, "Regionale Wachstumsdifferenzierung in Deutschland im 19. Jahrhundert unter besonderer Berücksichtigung des West-Ost-Gefälles," in *Wirtschaftliche und soziale Probleme der gewerblichen Entwicklung im 15./16. und 19. Jahrhundert*, ed. Friedrich Lütge (Stuttgart, 1968), pp. 115–30.
[41] See the book by Pollard cited above, note 25. For some examples of German multinational corporations, see Peter Hertner, *Fallstudien zu deutschen multinationalen Unternehmen vor dem Ersten Weltkrieg*, ed. N. Horn and J. Kocka (Göttingen, 1979), pp. 388–419.
[42] Characteristically, most research on the history of German women has focused on feminist politics, rather than on work or family life. See, for instance, Jean Quataert, *Reluctant Feminists in German Social*

which are clearly not national in their focus-recreational patterns, sexual behavior, demographic trends-we find that national aggregates can conceal as much as they reveal. This is one important lesson to be drawn from E. A. Wrigley's examination of the coal region of north-western Europe, which demonstrates how easily important demographic patterns can disappear in national averages. As Wrigley shows, the demography of the coal mining areas of France and Prussia tends to be more alike than either region is like its national norm.[43] Once we get away from the presuppositions and limitations built into abstractions like "German society," therefore, a whole range of new problems and possibilities becomes apparent.

As an analytical category, "German politics" certainly has more substance than "German economy," "German society," or "German culture." States are political entities, which have a real locus of power at their center. Here decisions are taken which can determine the fate of the national community. It would be unfortunate, therefore, if our search for new ways to view the past led us to ignore problems of state policy and power. Professor Goubert may well be right that in social life the region is the only reality because, as he puts it, "the French peasant is non-existent."[44] There are, however, French

---

Democracy, 1885–1917 (Princeton, 1979). For some samples of newer approaches, see the valuable collection edited by Werner Conze, *Sozialgeschichte der Familie in der Neuzeit Europas* (Stuttgart, 1976). An excellent survey of recent work on German social history can be found in P. Steinbach, "Alltagsleben und Landesgeschichte. Zur Kritik an einem neuen Forschungsinteresse," *Hessisches Jahrbuch für Landesgeschichte* 29 (1979): pp. 225–305.

[43] E. A. Wrigley, *Industrial Growth and Population Change* (Cambridge, 1961); see especially pp. 128 and 132–33 for a summary of the argument.

[44] Quoted by Michelle Perrot, "The Strengths and Weaknesses of French Social History, *Journal of Social History*, 10, no. 2 (1976): p. 167.

statesmen and generals. Their activities should never be dropped from a list of the historian's legitimate concerns.

But even in the political realm, we should be wary of false assumptions about institutional symmetry and cohesion. There almost always is, for instance, a big difference between the order given at the center and the way it is carried out on the periphery, a difference which does not usually become apparent if we confine our attention to the records of the central administration. Recent work on the Nazi period has underscored the value of contrasting the intentions of the policymaker and the performance of his agents.[45] The need to move away from the center is even more pressing in the history of participatory politics. After all, a great deal of the political activity that goes on at the national level is designed to simplify issues, to clarify alignments, to reduce politics to a set of binary choices. Our most readily accessible evidence is about this sort of activity-electoral data, parliamentary debates, official statements, and so on. But this activity at the center obscures as much as it reflects the political life of the nation, as we all know from our everyday experience. In the worlds of local politics, choices are frequently more fluid, alliances more uncertain, combinations more complex. Dick Geary's fine work on the differences between local and national alignments in Social Democracy illustrates just how important it is not to confuse national politics with German politics as a whole. It is not that local affairs are somehow more real or basic than national ones, but rather that they are often different. To recognize this difference is to take the first step toward the

---

It is remarkable that France, Europe's most centralized nation, has been dissolved by its historians into regions, while Germany, one of Europe's most fragmented polities, is treated as if it were a cohesive entity.

[45] Edward Peterson, *The Limits of Hitler's Power* (Princeton, 1969).

essential question of how various levels of political action relate to one another.[46]

What is German history from 1866 to 1945? It is, first of all, the history of the unified nation, of Bismarck's Germany, its origins and evolution, its economic, social, and cultural life, the loyalties it evoked, and the reasons for its destruction. But German history is also the history of experiences which do not fit within the boundaries of the nation, the history of cultural richness and regional diversity, of economic activities and social institutions without national configuration, of relationships which stretch across legally defined frontiers. Finally and most importantly, German history is the history of how these two sets of forces interacted, the history of a prolonged tension between unity and diversity, between the search for cohesion and the fact of fragmentation. To understand this tension helps us to understand why the promise of national unity had such power for so many Germans and why this promise never was fulfilled.[47]

---

[46] Dick Geary, "Radicalism and the Worker: Metalworkers and Revolution, 1914–1923," in *Society and Politics in Wilhelmine Germany*, ed. Richard Evans (New York, 1978).

[47] My point here is obviously related to Theodor Schieder's concept of "incompleteness," which he takes to be an essential feature of German national, constitutional, and cultural development: "Grundfragen der neueren deutschen Geschichte," *Historische Zeitschrift*, 192, no. 1 (1961): pp. 1–16. One thing about this concept worries me: to talk about "incompleteness" might seem to imply that somewhere, under some circumstances, completion *(Vollendung* is the much richer German word) might have been, or might still be, possible. This, I hope I have made clear, is most certainly not the case.

After I had finished drafting the present essay, I came across Richard Lowenthal's "Geschichtszerrissenheit und Geschichtsbewusstsein in Deutschland," *Reden und Ansprachen zur Eröffnung des Instituts fur Deutsche Geschichte an der Universität Tel Aviv*

If we remove the kleindeutsch Reich from its unique and privileged position as the subject of German history and put in its place the persistent struggle between cohesion and fragmentation, we gain not only a new view of the German past, but also a different perspective from which to examine the German present. From this perspective, we can see that 1945 did not mark "the end of German history," as some have mournfully proclaimed. Nor is German history after 1945 simply the history of the Federal Republic, the "real" Germany's temporarily truncated extension. These radical expressions of discontinuity and continuity are both misleading, because both define the postwar era in terms of the old Reich.[48] It is time to acknowledge that the present period has a historical legitimacy of its own, a legitimacy which comes not from its relationship to the old Reich, but from its place within a broader and deeper historical tradition. The German present is not a postscript to the imperial past; it is a new chapter in a much older story. This is, as I have tried to show, a story which transcends any single answer to the question of German identity but rather accepts as its subject the peculiar pains and promise of the question itself.

(Tel Aviv, 1972), pp. 13–29. As his title suggests, Lowenthal's purpose in this essay is similar to mine, although his formulation of the issues is quite different.

[48] For a striking example of how questionable this *kleindeutsch* residue appears from an Austrian perspective, see the sharp critique of the new edition of Gebhardt's *Handbuch der deutschen Geschichte* by two leading Austrian historians (Fritz Fellner and Georg E. Schmid, "Ende oder Epoche der deutschen Geschichte?," *Zeitgeschichte* 5 (1977–1978): pp. 158–71. I am grateful to Professor Fellner for bringing this article to my attention.

3

The Problem of the Nation in German History*

Let's try to achieve some precision in regards to these difficult questions, questions in which the least confusion over the meaning of words in the first steps of the reasoning process can produce by the end the most disastrous errors. What we are going to do is a delicate operation, indeed, it is nearly vivisection: we are going to treat the living as one ordinarily treats the dead. We shall keep them cold, however, with the most absolute impartiality.

Ernest Renan, "Qu'est-ce qu'une Nation?" (1882)[1]

In the rectoral address which he delivered at Göttingen almost exactly thirty years ago, Hermann Heimpel reflected on the contemporary problem of the German nation. "Talk about the nation," he said, has lost its "inner self-assurance, its freshness and sustaining naiveté." Like the concept of humanity, the concept of the nation has become so "uncertain and so tentative . . . that neither one nor the other could be confidently

---

*Originally published in *Die Rolle der Nation in der Deutschen Geschichte und Gegenwart*, eds. Otto Büsch and James J. Sheehan (Berlin, 1985), pp. 3–20.

[1] Renan, *Oeuvres complètes*, vol. 1 (Paris, n.d.), p. 888.

used to determine the historical subject any longer."[2] The pathos that Heimpel expressed was common in the late 1940's and early 1950's as German historians confronted the tragic condition of their nation, the burdens of its past, the uncertainties of its future.

But the particularly painful condition of the postwar German nation should not distract us from the fact that the concept of the nation is and always has been "uncertain" and "tentative." The German nation has never been easy to define, either historically or historiographically.

"All terms," Nietzsche once wrote, "which semiotically condense a whole process elude definition; only that which has no history can be defined."[3] We might apply Nietzsche's insight to our present purposes by pointing out that the concept of the nation resists definition because it has only history. Nations lack a definable core, an objective basis for their existence, an irreducible essence, a set of logically necessary characteristics. The biological metaphors which have so permeated most discussions of nations and nation building help to distract us from this fact. We talk about the "growth" of nations, about nations "becoming self–conscious," about a nation's "development" from cultural to political awareness. But nations do not grow like organisms, there is nothing natural about their evolution. They are all artifacts of human will.

The first step to an understanding of nations in history is to recognize that nations are invented—a term which strikes me as especially appropriate because it combines the idea of

---

[2] Heimpel, "Entwurf einer Deutschen Geschichte," in Heimpel, *Der Mensch in seiner Gegenwart* (Göttingen, 1954), pp. 172–73. For some general reflections on the concept of the nation in postwar German history, see Ernst Nolte, "Zur Konzeption der Nationalgeschichte heute," *Historische Zeitschrift*, 202, no. 3 (1966): pp. 603–21.

[3] Nietzsche, "The Genealogy of Morals," in *The Birth of Tragedy and the Genealogy of Morals* (New York, 1956), Part 2, Section 13, p. 212.

discovery with that of contrivance. To say that nations are invented does not mean that they are unreal or fictitious; obviously this is not so. But nations are products of history and therefore are invented in both senses of the word, as people discover and create the bonds of their nationality. Moreover, much of what is considered to be discovery turns out, upon closer examination, to have been created. For instance, the roots of national identity which people think they have discovered in the past often enough are newly–minted creations, fabricated to serve as the foundation for a future national community. Friedrich Schlegel may have had this point in mind when he wrote at the end of the eighteenth century: "Except for putting it in the wrong historical position, no fault is to be found with the archetype of Germanness proposed by some of the great national scholars. This Germanness does not lie behind us, but rather in front of us."[4]

There are at least two important reasons why the history of a nation's invention is very difficult to follow. First, it is obviously an extremely complicated story, involving changes in the distribution of social, economic, political, military, and cultural power. Intellectuals, businessmen, political leaders, and soldiers all have a role in this story– and not always the role they intended to play. Second, and more directly relevant to our present concerns, the history and historiography of nations are always intertwined. Historiography—in John Pocock's phrase—is "both the instrument and the record" of nation building.[5] The invention of the nation always involves the invention of a national past, an established version of the

---

[4] Schlegel, *Schriften zur Literatur*, ed. W. Rasch (Munich, 1972), p. 11. On the meaning of historical "invention," see the stimulating remarks in Bernard Lewis, *History: Remembered, Recovered, Invented* (Princeton, 1975).

[5] J. G. A. Pocock, "The Limits and Divisions of British History: In Search of the Unknown Subject," *American Historical Review*, 87, no. 2 (1982): p. 321.

nation's creation which absorbs or overwhelms alternative points of view. One of the essential features of such national history is the insistence that the nation is a natural entity whose political existence is necessary and inevitable. As a result, one cannot easily recover a sense of the contingencies and missed opportunities which every process of nation building involves.

The purpose of this paper is to examine the invention of the nation in German historiography. I shall do this by considering what I take to be the two fundamental convictions upon which the national interpretation of German history is based: first, that there is a German national community with a distinctive character and manifest historical existence, and second, that this community's search for political expression is the central theme of German history and the most important subject of German historiography.[6] The first of these convictions took shape during the late eighteenth century, the second during the middle decades of the nineteenth.

Considerations of time and space make it necessary for me to focus my attention on a few important individuals whose work best illustrates or most clearly reflects broader patterns and widely held assumptions. I want to insist, however, that these men did not invent the nation on their own. Their ideas about the nation and nationality took shape within, and drew their influence from, political conflicts. The historians whom I shall discuss here are significant because the vision of the nation they espoused won—politically and militarily as well as historiographically. And it was this political and military victory which gave them their apparently privileged position in the evolution of national historiography. Had the Prussians lost at

---

[6] I have adapted here the standard definition of nationalism as given by Elie Kedourie: Nationalism, he writes, "holds that humanity is naturally divided into nations, that nations are known by certain characteristics which can be ascertained, and that the only legitimate type of government is national self-government." *Nationalism* (London, 1960), p. 9.

Königgrätz, both the history of German politics and the politics of German historiography would have been different.

I. In the Beginning was the Volk

As has often been noted, one of the distinctive features of German national thought is the attempt to establish that "National belonging is not based on free volition, but rather on fate that is determined by nature and history."[7] Germans who hoped to establish a basis for their national identity have persistently looked for cultural characteristics, moral attributes, even physical traits, which were irrevocably theirs, entitlements by birth, inescapable transmissions from their ancestors. But since these sources of identity were by their nature elusive, difficult if not impossible to find in the real world, the best place to locate them was in the past, in some lineage which would link Germans to one another and clearly set them apart from everybody else. From the sixteenth century, when German humanists first tried to find the basis for a national identity in the story of the tribes described by Tacitus, the search for a German Volk has been a historical enterprise.[8]

The concept of a German Volk, whose first tentative outlines can be found in the Renaissance, took on its definitive shape in the eighteenth century. The key figure here, of course, was Herder, who provided the most intellectually powerful and

---

[7] Ernst-Wolfgang Böckenförde, "Die Einheit von nationaler und konstitutioneller politischer Bewegung im deutschen Frühliberalismus," in *Moderne deutsche Verfassungsgeschichte (1815–1918)* (Cologne, 1972), p. 27.

[8] On the discovery of Tacitus by German Humanists, see Frank Borchardt, *German Antiquity in Renaissance Myth* (Baltimore and London, 1971). Lewis Spitz has an account of humanist views on nationality in his *Conrad Celtis: The German Arch Humanist* (Cambridge, MA, 1957), especially Chapter 10.

influential statement of the Volk's nature and importance. More than any other single writer, Herder formulated the rich and resonant vocabulary of national commitment which still affects the way we think and talk about nationality and nationalism.

Human beings, Herder believed, were joined by a tissue of relationships to a series of communities, each with its unique and essential identity, what he called its "inner life force." These communities—which range from the individual family to the human race itself—are the source of our identity; they make us what we are. These communities can be influenced by external forces, but there is something hard and immutable at their core. This is especially true of the Volk, the highest and most important collectivity: nations, like families or individuals, can alter but not lose their basic nature. Therefore, Herder assures his readers, if one knows where to look, one can find the true character of the German community, a source of meaning and identity which has persisted through all the discontinuities of the nation's history and despite all the fragmentation so characteristic of the national experience.

> "For every people is a people: each has its own national developments as its language; to be sure, sometimes the region left an imprint on everyone, and sometimes extended only a mild haze, but this does not destroy the original shape of the nation."[9]

"Jedes Volk ist Volk"—"Every people is a people." Generations of German historians shared Herder's conviction and drew from it, as he did, the moral force and intellectual focus for their work. Karl Friedrich von Savigny, for instance, searched through the history of legal systems in order to find the hidden unities imposed by the character of the Volk. As he wrote in the first volume of his *Zeitschrift für geschichtliche*

---

[9] Johann Gottfried Herder, *Ideen zur Philosophie der Geschichte der Menschheit, Sämmtliche Werke*, ed. Bernhard Suphan (Berlin, 1887), vol. 13, pp. 257–58.

Rechtswissenschaft (1815), every set of laws and legal institutions has a Lebensprincip, from which all their diverse appearances derived; this principle was to be found historically, by painstaking retrospection through "all of its transformations, up to its emergence from the people's character, fate, and needs." Both as a patriot and a scholar, Savigny was committed to the idea that every nation had a law of its own, a tradition which reflected "an individuality that was not merely coincidental, but rather essential and necessary, based on its entire past." Like his former student and longtime friend, Jacob Grimm, Savigny did not think that the Volk was created by its laws or its language; rather the opposite was true, the Volk's hidden, secret character was revealed through these outward manifestations.[10]

It was not necessary to share Savigny's and Grimm's emotionally charged view of the Volk in order to believe that each nation had its own personality, fed from historical sources beyond the will of any individual. Everywhere we go, wrote Leopold von Ranke in *Das politische Gespräch* of 1836, our fatherland is "with us, inside of us. . . . We rest upon it from the beginning and cannot emancipate ourselves. This secret thing, . . . this spiritual air, . . . precedes every constitution and enlivens and fulfills all of its forms."[11] Three decades later, in his essay on "Die Deutschen bei ihrem Eintritt in die Geschichte," Heinrich von Sybel invoked virtues which he believed had always been part of Germans' public and private lives. "Over the centuries, we have grown and progressed— but today we are still what we were yesterday." Gustav Freytag

---

[10] Friedrich Karl von Savigny, "Recession." Nicolaus Thaddäus von Gönner, "Über Gesetzgebung und Rechtswissenschaft in unserer Zeit," *Zeitschrift für geschichtliche Rechtswissenschaft*, 1 (1815): pp. 395–96. For a comparison of historical methods of philologists and legal historians, see Mack Walker, *German Home Towns* (Ithaca, 1971).
[11] Leopold von Ranke, *Die grossen Mächte. Politisches Gespräch*, ed. Theodor Schieder (Göttingen, 1955), pp. 57–58.

agreed: he began the 1866 edition of his *Bilder aus der deutschen Vergangenheit* by saying that because Germans have changed much less since Roman times than one might think, it is still possible to hear exactly the same national heartbeat. Throughout history, Freytag believed, national character has asserted itself again and again.[12]

The conviction of historical continuity which Sybel and Freytag celebrated on the eve of the nation's triumph later consoled another generation at a time of national defeat. In the history of Germany which he wrote during the 1920's, Johannes Haller made the Volk his tragic hero, which struggled to sustain itself through the centuries against adversity and foreign antagonists. About the same time, Gerhard Ritter declared: "The meaning of German history seems . . . to lie in the idea that . . . we are the forever incomplete but forever striving, forever youthful nation, a nation that never stops becoming. . . . "[13] And finally, to take an example from close to our own time: Friedrich Meinecke, in his moving postwar reflections on "Ranke and Burckhardt," assured his readers that although "we Germans live today amid the ruins of state and nation . . . one thing has remained to us, our own German way of being men."[14]

For over two centuries, from Herder's time to Meinecke's, a remarkable consensus existed among German historians that there is a Volk, a distinctive historical collectivity upon whose foundation a national history might be erected. The persistence of this consensus is all the more remarkable when we consider

---

[12] Heinrich von Sybel, *Kleine historische Schriften*, 3 vols., (Munich, 1869–1880), vol. 1, p. 45; Gustav Freytag, *Bilder aus der deutschen Vergangenheit*, *Gesammelte Werke* (Leipzig, 1897–98), vol. 17, pp. i–ii.

[13] Cf. Bernd Faulenbach, *Ideologie des deutschen Wegs. Die deutsche Geschichte in der Historiographie zwischen Kaiserreich und Nationalsozialismus* (Munich, 1980), pp. 27, 31–32.

[14] Friedrich Meinecke, "Ranke and Burckhardt," in Hans Kohn, ed., *German History: Some New German Views* (Boston, 1954), p. 156.

that while the concept of the Volk may have profound psychological force and important political implications, its empirical utility is extremely limited. Herder, one of its most important inventors, contributed to both the theory of the nation and the theory of history, but he did not write much national history. In Leonard Krieger's telling phrase, among his contemporaries Herder "came closest to being a nationalist [but] was furthest from being a historian."[15] Savigny and Grimm did distinguished work on the history of language and of law but never found those mystical bonds of community which they believed were the taproot of nationality. Indeed, when we look at their books, we find that the Volk turns out to be the occasion for, not the subject of, their scholarly endeavors. Ranke, Sybel, and their contemporaries may have believed firmly in the Volk's existence, but their attention as historians was focused elsewhere, on more empirically accessible issues and institutions. Nor have more recent efforts to ground the Volk scientifically been especially successful. We can pass quickly over the biological theories of nationality whose sinister effects are known to all of us. The concept of "national character," which turns out to be the romantic presumption of the Volk in social scientific guise, has not proved to be an effective basis for research. Mercifully, its vogue seems to have passed.

We need not spend much time disproving the existence of the Volk in either its traditional or pseudoscientific formulations. However, two points are worth mentioning about the conceptual history of the Volk. First, the uses of the Volk were always shaped by political struggles and aspirations. Herder, for instance, used his notion of nationality as a weapon against the influence of French culture and its advocates among the court nobility, just as national thinkers a generation

---

[15] Leonard Krieger, "Germany," in Orest Ranum, ed., *National Consciousness, History, and Political Culture in Early Modern Europe* (Baltimore, 1975), p. 69.

later used the Volk against the influence of the French conquerors and their German allies.[16] Second, there was always a disjunction between the concept of the Volk and the reality it was supposed to describe. As Ernest Gellner has reminded us, there is an "inverse relationship between the ideology and the reality of nationalism. The self image of nationalism involves the stress on folk, folklore, popular culture, etc. In fact, nationalism becomes important precisely when these things become artificial."[17] Concepts of nationality are the products of historical change not the reflections of historical continuity.

II. *The Volk and the Staat*

To Herder, Volk and state belonged to different realms, the one authentic, historic, humane, the other, mechanical, contrived, imposed upon men. "Statesmen may deceive one another," he wrote in 1764, "political machines may be positioned against one another, until one blows the other one up. But nations do not confront one another like that; they calmly lie side by side and support each other like families." German history was not the history of political machines, dynasties, or princes; it had to do with "the German nation, its constitution, welfare, and language."[18] In the first decades of the nineteenth century, however, a number of Germans came to believe that their nation's "constitution, welfare, and

---

[16] There are some stimulating comments on the political uses of national concepts in Klaus von See, *Deutsche Germanen-Ideologie* (Frankfurt, 1970).

[17] Ernest Gellner, *Thought and Change* (Chicago, 1964), p. 162.

[18] The first quotation from Herder is in Günter List, "Historische Theorie und nationale Geschichte zwischen Frühliberalismus und Reichgründung," in Bernd Faulenbach, ed., *Geschichtswissenschaft in Deutschland* (Munich, 1974), p. 35; the second in *Sämmliche Werke*, vol. 18, pp. 382–83.

language" could only be realized through the power of the state. In time, state and nation were seen as inseparable, the one drawing its power and legitimacy from the other. By mid-century, many historians were convinced that a national state was the most mature stage in the life of a Volk, the proper destination in its journey towards self-expression. As Georg Waitz put it in 1862: "The natural bond of the people . . . reaches its completion when it is embodied in a state." This conviction became the basis of what can be called the national interpretation of history, which assumes that nations progress from idea to reality, from culture to politics, from Herder's Volk to Bismarck's Reich. "The national spirit," wrote Otto Hintze in 1903, "which has reached consciousness, demands its body: the state."[19]

This interpretation has become so deeply entrenched in our thinking that we often underestimate the profound difficulty German historians have always had putting together the state and the Volk. Savigny, for instance, who belonged to that generation of patriots mobilized during the revolutionary wars, was very uncertain about the political form his patriotic longings should assume. The source of his love for the fatherland, and for his hatred of the French, was not some future nation state but rather the traditions of the past, the Germans' laws and customs as they had been realized in various regions, cities, and states. As he made apparent in his famous polemic against Thibaut, Savigny opposed a premature unification of German legal institutions, preferring instead the gradual emergence of institutional unity through a careful study of the past.[20] Jacob Grimm—whose patriotic credentials are

---

[19] Georg Waitz quoted in Böckenförde, ed., "Die Einheit" (see note 7 above), p. 35, note 10; Otto Hintze, in Hans Herzfeld, "Staat und Nation in der deutschen Geschichtsschreibung der Weimarer Zeit," in Herzfeld, *Ausgewählte Aufsätze* (Berlin, 1962), pp. 63–64.

[20] Jacques Stern, ed., *Thibaut und Savigny* (Munich, 1973), provides the main documents in this debate. On Savigny's view of the nation, see

certainly genuine enough—was also uncertain about the
implications of his national feelings. In his Antrittsrede of
1830, "De desiderio patriae," he praised the fatherland in all its
forms, local, national, and cultural. As he wrote to his friend
Lachmann: "Secretly, my desiderium patriae also includes
Hesse, even though I focused on Germany and the German
language."[21]

Perhaps the most explicit statement of the problems in
finding a relationship between Volk and state is to be found in
Ranke's dialogue on politics. Ranke, as we have seen, believed
that national identity was an attribute we could not deny; he
was also persuaded that nationalism was a powerful political
force in modern times. Yet he recognized that states and
nations do not easily coexist: "Nations tend towards statehood,
but I do not know a single nation that truly is a state. . . . States
are by their nature much more narrowly enclosed than nations;
they modify both human and national existence."[22]

Ranke was not especially troubled by the imperfect
relationship between Volk and state. Since he did not believe
in popular sovereignty and was suspicious of patriotic excess,
he was perfectly willing to acknowledge the centrality and
priority of the state, both in his politics and in his scholarship.
To Ranke's liberal contemporaries, however, the question of
Volk und Staat relations could not be so easily resolved. For
them, the Volk was a central political value, the source of their
own legitimacy as a movement, the ultimate goal of their
political endeavors. During the middle decades of the
nineteenth century—the decisive era in both history and

---

the stimulating remarks in Werner Kaegi, "Geschichtswissenschaft
und Staat in der Zeit Rankes," in Kaegi, *Historische Meditationen*
(Zurich, 1946), vol. 2, p. 132.

[21] *Briefwechsel der Brüder Jacob und Wilhelm Grimm mit Karl Lachmann*, 2
vols. (Jena, 1927), vol. 2, p. 552. In the essay cited in note 20, Kaegi
discusses Grimm's ideas on pp. 133–34.

[22] Ranke, *Die grossen Mächte* (note 11 above), p. 58.

historiography—it became politically and intellectually essential for liberal historians to create a version of the German past in and through which Volk and Staat might be reconciled. The national interpretation of German history was formed during a series of bitter struggles over Germany's future between the liberals and their enemies.[23] Clearly this struggle is much too complex for us to follow here. We will have to be content with a single illustration, the work of Johann Gustav Droysen, whom Heinrich von Srbik regarded as the "true founder and creator of the Prussian kleindeutsch school."

After writing a series of extraordinary studies of the ancient world, Droysen turned to modern history with his *Vorlesungen über das Zeitalter der Freiheitskriege*, which he delivered at Kiel in 1842/43 and published three years later. The lectures covered the entire period from 1770 to 1815, but as the title suggests, the highpoint of the narrative was marked by those "unforgettable years [. . .] during which, for the first time in centuries, the German people, carried by the celebration of its unity, fought and triumphed together." However it was not only the mobilization of the Volk that gave these years their historical significance and exemplary power. Equally important, for Droysen, and for the generations of historians who followed his interpretation, was the way in which the wars of liberation expressed a partnership between Volk and state, a partnership rooted in the era of Prussian reforms and then gloriously triumphant on the field of battle. "From then on," Droysen wrote, "to be a true state means to be a national state, and to be a true Volk means to be embodied in a state"—a concise statement of the interpretation which would make the

---

[23] There is a good summary of this process in List's essay (see note 18). See also Wolfgang Hardtwig, "Von Preussens Aufgabe in Deutschland zu Deutschlands Aufgabe in der Welt," *Historische Zeitschrift*, 231, no. 1 (1980): 265–324.

wars against Napoleon into one of the national interpretation of German history's central myths.[24]

The problem was, of course, that "from then on" the state did not become national, nor did the Volk achieve its state. Liberal historians, like liberal politicians, had to come to terms with the fact that the promise of the Freiheitskriege was not fulfilled. Volk and Staat were not so easily reconciled, practically, ideologically, or historiographically.

The effects of this on Droysen were clear and exemplary. Although he remained a liberal in politics and retained a deep commitment to the Volk as a "natural community," Droysen eventually recognized that Volk and Staat would rarely coincide. In his lectures of 1857, known as the Historik, he pointed out that the "history of peoples" would almost always be very different from the "history of states." An important part of the "lively movement" in history comes from the fact that they do not match, but continue to seek one another, the Volk eager for its "political representation," the state anxious to turn its inhabitants into a Volk, that is, "a substantial community."[25] In practice, Droysen's scholarly attention came to be more and more absorbed by the second of these processes: from the 1850's until his death, he devoted himself to a history of Prussia, a multivolume monument to the state which gave "to one side of our national life its expression, representation, and extent."[26] At the same time, his political values came to be increasingly centered on the state, which he viewed as a community with a life of its own, existing, like the Volk, beyond the will of those who live within it: "The state,"

---

[24] J. G. Droysen, *Vorlesungen über das Zeitalter der Freiheitskriege*, 2 vols., 2nd ed. (Gotha, 1886), vol. 1, p. 3, and vol. 2, p. 457.

[25] Droysen, *Historik: Historische-kritische Ausgabe*, ed. Peter Leyh (Stuttgart-Bad Cannstatt, 1977), p. 307.

[26] Droysen, *Geschichte der preussischen Politik* (1st ed. published from 1855 to 1886). The quotation is from the second edition (Leipzig, 1868 ff.), vol. 1, p. 3.

he wrote in the last version of the *Historik*, "is not the sum of the individuals it encompasses, nor does it arise from their will, nor does it exist for them."[27]

By the 1850's and 1860's, as the struggle over central Europe was entering its decisive phase, a number of other historians had followed Droysen's campaign against Napoleon and had anticipated and justified France's eventual domination over Germany. Similarly, Heinrich von Sybel, Ranke's most gifted student, established himself in Munich from where he advocated the creation of a nation state purged of its "non-German" elements—by which he meant Austria.[28]

It would be a mistake, however, to overestimate the predominance of this kleindeutsch viewpoint before 1866. One of the effects of the kleindeutsch triumph has been to reduce the historiography of the fifties and sixties to the story of its own creation, ignoring or pushing to one side the rich variety of historiographical—and, one might add, of political—alternatives which continued to exist. Georg Gervinus, for instance, tried to keep alive his faith in what he called the "tenacious and healthy national character." This, he hoped, would provide a basis for German politics without "the dangerously homogenous large states."[29] A similar concern to avoid the primacy of a hegemonical state informed Wilhelm von Giesebrecht's *Geschichte der deutschen Kaiserzeit* of 1855, which tried to create a more positive image of the old empire. Julius von Ficker's attempt to defend Giesebrecht's views from Sybel's critical attack triggered one of the last great

---

[27] Droysen, *Historik*, p. 441.

[28] Ludwig Häusser, *Deutsche Geschichte vom Tode Friedrichs des Grossen bis zur Gründung des Deutschen Bundes*, 4 vols., 2nd ed. (Berlin, 1854–63). There is fine account of Sybel's career in Volker Dotterweich, *Heinrich von Sybel. Geschichtswissenschaft in politischer Absicht (1817–1861)* (Göttingen, 1978).

[29] Georg Gervinus, *Einleitung in die Geschichte des neunzehnten Jahrhunderts*, ed. Walter Boehlich (Frankfurt, 1967), p. 178.

historiographical controversies before the formation of the
Bismarckian Reich.[30]

The point of mentioning historians like Gervinus and
Ficker is not to suggest that they had better answers to the
relationship between Volk and Staat than did Droysen and
Sybel. Politically that may be true; historiographically it is by
no means certain. There are, I think, some real problems
involved in trying to define "German history" according to the
models suggested by either Gervinus or Ficker. But there are
problems in every definition of the German past. Neither
kleindeutsch nor grossdeutsch, neither the primacy of the state
nor the primacy of the Volk provides us with a natural,
privileged answer to the relationship between German culture
and German politics, between the nation and the state.[31]

The answer offered by Droysen and his colleagues seemed
obvious, natural, and privileged once the issue was settled
politically and militarily. At that point, after Königgrätz, the
Prussian solution came to seem retrospectively what it had
become practically: irresistible. Now, as Treitschke put it in
1866: "Prussian and German history absolutely had to be one
common creation." The link between Volk and Staat had been
forged, the historical arch between Herder and Bismarck had
been closed. "Using the power of the Prussian state, Bismarck

---

[30] G. Koch, "Der Streit zwischen Sybel und Ficker um die
Einschätzung der mittelalterlichen Kaiserpolitik in der modernen
Historiographie," in J. Streisand, ed., *Studien über die deutsche
Geschichtswissenschaft*, 2 vols. (Berlin, 1963), vol. 1, pp. 311–38.

[31] The easiest way to grasp the problematic character of the
kleindeutsch answer is by viewing German history from an Austrian
perspective: see, for example, Friedrich Heer, *Der Kampf um die
österreichische Identität* (Vienna, 1981). I am grateful to Fritz Fellner for
providing me with the manuscript of his essay on "Die
Historiographie zur österreichisch-deutschen Problematik als
Spiegel der nationalpolitischen Diskussion," which also illuminates
this issue.

realized the idea of the German nation. The new German Empire was at once power and idea." Meinecke's summary phrase captures the essence of the path which led to a belief in the primacy of the Prussian state. Ludwig Häusser's history of the revolutionary era was even more Prussocentric than Droysen's had been; to Häusser, Prussia's leadership in the kleindeutsch interpretation of German history, an interpretation which merges idea and power, Volk and Staat, Prussia and Germany.[32]

In the years after 1866, the kleindeutsch interpretation came to dominate both academic and popular images of the German past. It was enshrined in paintings and sculptures, reinforced in national ceremonies, taught in the schools, and adopted without question by the historical profession. Elizabeth Fehrenbach's remark that there was no nineteenth-century "counter-narrative to Sybel's kleindeutsch conception of history" holds true for the twentieth century as well.[33] Even a book such as Srbik's *Deutsche Einheit*, often portrayed as an alternative to the national interpretation, is only a modification of the established viewpoint. Srbik did not doubt the existence of the German Volk and accepted its natural evolution towards nationhood. He simply wanted the process to continue until it included the rest of German-speaking Europe—a position many kleindeutsch historians adopted without difficulty when such a possibility presented itself in the 1930's.[34]

---

[32] Treitschke is quoted in Ernst Schulin, *Traditionskritik und Rekonstruktionsversuch. Studien zur Entwicklung von Geschichtswissenschaft und historischem Denken* (Göttingen, 1979), p. 82; Friedrich Meinecke, "Reich und Nation von 1871–1914," in Meinecke, *Staat und Persönlichkeit* (Berlin, 1933), p. 165.

[33] Fehrenbach, "Die Reichsgründung in der deutschen Geschichtsschreibung," in Theodor Schieder and Ernst Deuerlein, eds., *Reichsgründung 1870/71* (Stuttgart, 1970), p. 265.

[34] On this point, see the work of B. Faulenbach, cited above in note 13.

The kleindeutsch interpretation triumphed because it seemed to fit people's political experience and because it was backed by the power of the state. The writing of national history is, to quote again the phrase by John Pocock I used earlier, the "instrument" as well as the "record" of nation building.

III. *Conclusion*

Like other official versions of national history, the kleindeutsch interpretation was extremely flexible and adaptable. It shaped historians' approach to every facet of the past, imposing a kleindeutsch solution on the history of philosophy, literature, science, and socioeconomic life. Gustav von Schmoller and his many followers used it to understand the development of German economics; Meinecke saw it as a key to the history of ideas; Karl Lamprecht had no trouble reconciling his views on culture with a commitment to the nation state. Furthermore, the national interpretation has been able to accommodate a variety of political viewpoints, ranging from the far left to the far right, including conservatives and Marxists, moderate liberals and radical republicans. In short, the kleindeutsch interpretation is not a particular school of history, but rather provides a mode of discourse within which various interpretations are debated. Long ago detached from its original ideological moorings, it is now the idiom which different parties can use to express their disagreements.

The ubiquity and pliability of this interpretation remind us of the "Whig interpretation" of English history so brilliantly defined by Herbert Butterfield. Like the whig interpretation, it has become an ordering model of national identity, whose influence is "much more subtle than mental bias; it lies in the trick of organization, an unexamined habit of mind that any historian may fall into."[35] The kleindeutsch interpretation is too deeply embedded in our working assumptions to be visible to the naked eye. It has become a hidden feature of our intellectual landscape, so familiar that we miss the ways its contours shape the explanatory structures we try to build upon it.

There is no point in trying to prove or disprove such interpretations. In an important sense, these ordering myths of a nation's identity are beyond considerations of truth or falsehood—they are simply there, part of our physical and mental cartography, the units in which much of our evidence is gathered and published, an indelible imprint on our language. However, like every historical interpretation, these national views of history highlight some subjects and obscure others, make us aware of certain kinds of problems and distract us from those which do not fit within their intellectual boundaries. At the very least, it seems to me prudent to be aware of these boundaries and especially of the issues which lie beyond them.[36]

Paradoxically perhaps, the kleindeutsch interpretation is most obviously vulnerable in the area where national historiography first developed: cultural life. German culture has always been too rich and complex to coincide with the borders of a nation state. Popular cultures have characteristically followed the lines drawn by regional or group identities, only rarely those of statesmen. High culture has

---

[35] Butterfield, *The Whig Interpretation of History* (London, 1959), p. 30. I wish that we had an analysis of the national interpretation of German history as rich and suggestive as John Burrow's *A Liberal Descent: Victorian Historians and the English Past* (Cambridge, 1981).

[36] I have explored these issues at somewhat greater length in my essay "What is German History? Reflections on the Role of the Nation in German History and Historiography," *Journal of Modern History*, 53, no. 1 (1981): pp. 1–23.

often been too universal to fit within a state, or else it has radiated out from local centers across boundaries and within regional networks. It is not difficult to compile a list of creative individuals who have never lived in what is usually called "Germany," but who have nourished, and been nourished by, the magnificence of the German language and its literary accomplishments. Let Grillparzer speak for all these people:

> Als Deutscher ward ich geboren —
> Bin ich noch einer?
> Nur was ich Deutsches geschrieben,
> Das nimmt mir keiner.

I think the limitations of the kleindeutsch interpretation are no less apparent in the realm of social and economic history. Tipton's fine critical analysis of the national approach to economic development has recently been followed by a series of empirical studies which affirm the importance of regional and transnational economic institutions. In a book which strikes me as of particular interest to students of German affairs, Sidney Pollard has demonstrated the drawbacks of dividing Europe into national economic units. Finally, Wrigley's pioneering study of demographic patterns in the adjoining coal regions of Germany, France, and Belgium shows us how easily regional conditions can be lost from sight when they are absorbed into national averages.[37] Obviously the nation state has a significant impact on society and economics; perhaps this impact has increased in the past two centuries. But to appreciate the nation's social and economic role we must study both supranational and regional units. Above all we must be aware that all nations "consist of an amalgam of fragments," which cannot be too swiftly aggregated. There are always

---

[37] Frank Tipton, "The National Consensus in German Economic History," *Central European History*, 7, no. 3 (1974): pp. 195–224; Sidney Pollard, *Peaceful Conquest: The Industrialization of Europe, 1760–1970* (Oxford, 1981); E. A. Wrigley, *Industrial Growth and Population Change* (Cambridge, 1961).

frontiers which do not appear on the maps our political leaders provide: to understand these frontiers, we must, as Lucien Febvre has admonished us, start our investigations "from the inside, never from the outside."[38]

It is not difficult to see those cultural, social, and economic dimensions of life which do not conform to the politically imposed boundaries of the nation state. All we have to do is to consider the fecund diversity of life in central Europe, whose monuments and manifestations are plain to see all around us. It is much more difficult, however, to conceive of a politics outside the nation state—politics was, after all, the kleindeutsch interpretation's original terrain, its primary subject and the ultimate source of its influence. Is it possible to move beyond this interpretation in the political realm and to define a politics which would be flexible enough to embrace a wide range of human experiences, yet concrete enough to serve as the basis for empirical research? Can we, in other words, find a German politics which is not inexorably tied to the history of a single German nation state?

Such a politics could not exclusively focus on constitutional issues and formal political institutions—matters which lead one naturally back to the nation state. It would have to consider those conflicts and configurations which exist outside of what we usually define as politics, struggles for authority and power in schools and churches, workplaces and communities, law courts and local government. Equally important, this new vision of politics would have to be pluralistic. It could not be kleindeutsch or grossdeutsch, unitary or particularistic—all of these alternatives can only be debated within the prevailing interpretation. Our object should be to get outside of it, to consider the way in which various regions and groups and states have sought to retain or acquire influence, to grasp what

---

[38] Lucien Febvre and Lionell Bataillon, *A Geographical Introduction to History* (London and New York, 1925), pp. 309 and 311.

has always been the multilateral network of political relationships within central Europe.

The difficulties in defining such a politics are profound—much too profound to be treated in a paper like this one. But since the difficulties are so obvious, it seems worthwhile to underscore the advantages such a view of politics might bring to our understanding of the German past. First, it would enable us to study cultural, social, and economic problems without confining ourselves to national units or ignoring political concerns. This could, I think, help us to avoid that most unfortunate tendency to depoliticize the study of society and economics which a number of scholars have recently warned us against. Second, a multilateral view of German politics would give us a perspective from which we could study German history before 1866 and after 1945 as part of a continuous process. As long as the nation state remains our model and norm, it is difficult to avoid treating these periods as prologue or aftermath.[39]

In conclusion, let me return to the quotation from Hermann Heimpel with which I began. It seems to me that while Heimpel's remarks about the instability and uncertainty of the nation have a particular meaning for postwar Germany, they apply to every nation state. Some nations have had a more fortunate history than others, some have been blessed by circumstance or geography, but all of them have been invented, all are products of particular political forces, and all are to some degree problematic. There are signs that this perspective is becoming increasingly apparent to historians and social scientists in several different countries. Not long ago, for

---

[39] In rather different ways, Mack Walker's *German Home Towns* (see note 10) and Heinrich Lutz's recent essays try to provide perspectives from which the continuities as well as the breaks in German history can be observed: see Lutz, *Die Deutsche Nation zu Beginn der Neuzeit* (Munich, 1982).

example, David Hollinger raised the same point about American culture that I tried to suggest about Germany:

> The question of "America" . . . has antithetical local and cosmopolitan dimensions: particularism within and universalism without have drawn upon the intellectual energies of Americans and recognition of this fact has made the concept of "America" less central, analytically, than it once was.[40]

From a somewhat similar perspective, LeBras and Todd, in a work significantly entitled *L'Invention de la France*, have maintained that despite its apparent historical unity, France is a composite of quite distinct cultural entities: "Each of the regions of France represents a culture . . . that is to say a way of living and dying, an ensemble of rules defining human relationships . . . "[41] And finally, to cite the work of someone who has greatly influenced my own thinking, John Pocock recently tried to find a new meaning for British history, which would be "a plural history, tracing the processes by which a diversity of societies, nationalities, and political structures came into being and . . . the processes that have led them to whatever forms of association or unity exist in the present or have existed in the past."[42]

Hollinger, Todd and LeBras, and Pocock, like Heimpel, all write under the influence of the nation's changing political role in the postwar world. From what we know of nineteenth century historiography, it would be surprising if changes in the political present did not affect the way we view the past. Of course, contrary to what many hoped or feared in the late 1940's and 1950's, the era of the nation state has not come to an end. Although it has been absorbed into supranational alliance systems and is often threatened by newly awakened

---

[40] Hollinger, *Reviews in American History*, 10, no. 4 (1982): p. 310.

[41] H. LeBras and E. Todd, *L'Invention de la France. Atlas anthropologique et politique* (Paris,1981), p. 7.

[42] Pocock, "Limits and Divisions of British History" (cited in note 5), p. 320.

regional movements, the nation state survives and there is little sign that it will not continue to do so.

Nevertheless, we have learned enough, I believe, not to take the nation state for granted, either as a way of organizing our public life or as a means of organizing our study of the past. It may be that we can and should do no more than recognize the nation's political and conceptual limitations—but even that recognition would help us to recover what Herbert Butterfield once called the "elasticity of mind" which is so often lost when we become "too enslaved to the past" and thus allow our deeply rooted assumptions to remain unexamined.[43]

---

[43] Butterfield, *The Englishman and His History* (first published in 1944, new edition, Hamden, CT, 1970), pp. 107–8.

4

National History and National Identity
in the New Germany*

In the late afternoon of 16 June 1904, Leopold Bloom, a small businessman of Jewish extraction, dropped into Barney Kiernan's public house in search of some light refreshment. Not surprising in an establishment of this sort in Dublin, the talk was of politics; it was led by a sinister, one-eyed man known as "The Citizen," who extolled the virtues of Ireland and the villainy of Britain in a style best imagined after several pints of Guinness. Into this overheated atmosphere Bloom brought an unwelcome hint of reason and good sense:

> —Persecution, says he, all the history of the world is full of it. Perpetuating national hatred among nations.

*Published in the *German Studies Review*, 15 (Winter 1992): pp. 163–74. The essay was first written as an address to the German Studies Association annual meeting in Los Angeles, September 1991. An earlier version was published as "Zukünftige Vergangenheit. Das deutsche Geschichtsbild in den neunziger Jahren," *Das historische Museum*, eds. G. Korff and M. Roth (Frankfurt and New York 1990), pp. 277–86. For some different reflections on "the future of the German past," formulated before unification, see the special issue of *Central European History*, 20, no. 3/4 (September/December 1989), eds. Michael Geyer and Konrad Jarausch.

—But do you know what a nation means? says John Wyse.

—Yes, says Bloom.

—What is it, says John Wyse.

—A nation? says Bloom. A nation is the same people living in the same place.

—By God, then, says Ned [one of the denizens of the pub], laughing, if that's so, I'm a nation for I'm living in the same place for the past five years.

So of course everyone had the laugh at Bloom and says he, trying to muck out of it:

—Or living in another place.

—That covers my case, says Joe.

—What is your nation if I may ask? says the citizen.

—Ireland, says Bloom. I was born here. Ireland.

To which the citizen responds by spitting on the floor, an action described with a vividness that has no place in a scholarly journal.[1]

I begin with this passage from Chapter 12—the so-called Cyclops episode—of *Ulysses* not only because it reminds us that problems of national identity are by no means peculiarly German, but also because I think Joyce provides us with a useful typology of the definitions of nationhood.

The first—and it is the one to which Bloom, a sensible man, is instinctively drawn—is a legal, objective definition: a nation is composed of those living in a particular state. But Bloom, like so many sensible people, is easily shaken by those less sensible than he. Moreover, his initial definition, which seemed to him so reasonable, does not quite fit the groups he himself represents: neither the Jews nor the Irish then had a state of their own, both were in different ways peoples of a diaspora. He moves, therefore, to a second definition, which is subjective and cultural: a nation is composed of those living in

<hr>

[1] James Joyce, *Ulysses* (New York, 1986), pp. 271–72.

different places, but believing somehow that they belong together. If the legal definition is best described in the third person—"he or she belongs," this cultural definition is best asserted in the first person—"I belong." Appropriately enough, the Citizen—whose one eye is supposed to alert us to his fanatical vision—introduces a third definition, which is normative and prescriptive. In this definition, legal residence and cultural identity are not enough; one must also possess certain characteristics—moral, ideological, perhaps racial— that qualify for membership. This definition is prescribed in the second person: you do or—as the Citizen implies in Bloom's case—you do not belong.

The development of most modern nationalisms can be seen as the prolonged effort to fuse these three definitions, that is, the prolonged effort to create a state that would contain all those who could and should be members. National history plays a central role in this process: states as legal entities can, at least in theory, exist without a past; but national cultures and, even more insistently, national norms require historical definition, justification, and defense. As we should expect, the air in Barney Kiernan's was as thick with history as it was with the smell of beer.[2]

This interaction of history and nationalism had a special place in the German world. As Isaiah Berlin pointed out in his splendid essay on Herder, the very language of nationality was invented by Germans in the eighteenth century. Other scholars have shown how this language shaped Germans' search for nationhood in the nineteenth century and how, after the nation was created, normative definitions of nationalism were used as a political weapon, to weaken, isolate, and eventually to destroy

---

[2] My views on national identity have been especially informed by Ernest Gellner, *Nations and Nationalism* (Ithaca, 1983) and Benedict Anderson, *Imagined Communities: Reflections on the Origins and Spread of Nationalism* (London, 1983).

those who were regarded as not being "really German." I mention these familiar facts because they provide the essential backdrop to the main subjects of this essay: first, the deeply problematic relationship between history and identity in the two German states in the postwar period, and second, the future of that relationship now that these two states have, once again, become a single nation.[3]

In all three meanings of nation, 1945 was catastrophic for Germans' national existence. The total defeat and unconditional surrender of the Nazi regime brought the German state to an end as a legal entity; the massive upheavals and population movements that had resulted from the expansion and then the contraction of German power shattered the social and political basis of German culture throughout central and eastern Europe; and finally, the extraordinary crimes committed by Germans and their allies obliterated those claims to moral and cultural superiority which has always been part of German national rhetoric. As a political, cultural, and moral entity, the nation created in 1871 was in ruins. If, as one historian had proclaimed in the 1920s, "Either we have Bismarck's Germany or no Germany at all— Kleindeutschland or Keindeutschland," then German history in 1945 had come to a stop.[4] And there were those who suggested that it had—in the immediate postwar years, some Germans referred to the "loss of history" by which they meant a fundamental break between past and present.

---

[3] I have struggled with the relationship between history and identity in two previous essays: "What is German History? Reflections on the Role of the Nation in German History and Historiography," *Journal of Modern History*, 53, no. 1 (March 1981): pp. 1–23, and "The Problem of the Nation in German History," in *Die Rolle der Nation in der deutschen Geschichte und Gegenwart*, eds. Otto Büsch and James Sheehan (Berlin, 1985), pp. 3–20.

[4] Erich Marcks, quoted in Bernd Faulenbach, *Ideologie des deutschen Weges* (Munich, 1980), p. 69.

And yet such breaks are impossible: neither individuals nor groups can sever their connections to the past. History does not stop, the power of memory cannot be denied, the search for identity goes on; and, as we all know, this was especially the case in postwar Germany, where one came upon—I am tempted to say, stumbled over—the past again and again, not only in novels and films, but in the lives of everyone one met. The lines of continuity between present and past may often have been obscure, but the past was always powerfully present.

Both of the states built on and from the ruins of the Reich had to create their political, cultural, and moral identities under the shadow of this ever present past. As we should expect, the German Democratic Republic and the Federal Republic chose very different ways of dealing with the painful legacies of their common history.

Officially, the GDR presented itself as the heir not of German history as a whole, but of its progressive forces, forces that had always resisted the counterforces of reaction and repression. In other words, the GDR rested its claim to national identity on a moral rather than legal or cultural basis. On this moral basis, which had its social location in the working class and its political instrument in the SED, a new, democratic Germany could be built. An essential expression of this moral claim was antifascism, which served to distance the regime from the German past and to empower its attacks on those allies and heirs of fascism who continued to flourish in the West.

One got a fine sense of this view of German history in the old Museum for German History whose exhibits once occupied the Zeughaus in East Berlin. These exhibits began with the first human settlements on German soil and continued to the present. In the early sections, the emphasis was on changing modes of production, the driving forces of historical change. Increasingly, one saw the progressive forces at work: the Protestant reformers—especially radical reformers like Thomas Münzer—peasant rebels, German Jacobins, the

labor movement, and of course, the German Communist
Party. In contrast to the powerful continuities that linked these
exhibits, the section on the period 1933-45 was oddly
incomplete and fragmentary. The Nazis, who appear as the
tools of capitalists and militarists, were treated very sketchily—
there was little about the social basis of the movement, its
popular support, or even the full implications of its repression
and brutality. Instead, there was a great deal about the
Communist resistance and the liberating Soviet army, the two
forces upon which the GDR was built. It would have been very
difficult to come away from this exhibition with the knowledge
that German "fascism" was passively tolerated by an
overwhelming majority of the German population and ardently
supported by a significant minority.

The political power and historical weakness of the GDR's
concept of fascism were joined at the root: anti-fascism may
have been an effective way to solidify an international alliance
of communist states against an international coalition of
fascists and capitalists, but it was not much use in trying to
understand the distinctively German features of National
Socialism. And this failure in historical understanding left a
perplexing gap between the GDR and the national past.[5]

As long as the GDR hoped to be the core of a united
Germany, its view of German history was negative and
narrowly moralistic. By the end of the 1960s, however, these
hopes had been replaced by the need to create a separate,
socialist state. One result of this was a somewhat more positive
view of German history. The definition of what might count
as a "progressive" historical force became rather more
spacious: some historical buildings were restored, Frederick
the Great's statue returned to Unter den Linden, the Luther
Year was duly celebrated. Nevertheless, the GDR's

<hr>

[5] See Konrad Jarausch, "The Failure of East German Antifascism:
Some Ironies of History as Politics," *German Studies Review*, 14, no. 1
(February 1991): pp. 85–102.

relationship to the German past remained largely negative, its continuity with German historical identity uneven and problematic. Increasingly, the leaders of the GDR seemed to have recognized that its historical identity would have to be created from its own history as an independent state; we see evidence of this in a series of scholarly projects and, ironically enough, in the carefully arranged celebrations of the state's fortieth anniversary, which took place in the fall of 1989. That the GDR had failed to create a convincing historical identity became painfully apparent even before the echoes of this celebration had died away.[6]

The Federal Republic's relationship to German history was no less problematic, but it was problematic in a different way. West Germany both was and was not the heir of the nation created in 1871. On the one hand, the Bonn government presented itself as the only legitimate successor to the Germany nation state; as its Preamble makes clear, the Republic's Basic Law was promulgated for the entire German Volk, including those who could not participate. Article 116 explicitly denied Leopold Bloom's first definition of nation: citizenship in the Federal Republic was not limited to those within its own borders, but was granted to anyone who had been a citizen of Germany on 31 December 1937—and to their descendants. This made Germany into a diaspora nation by including those—as Bloom put it—"living in another place." On the other hand, however, the Federal Republic represented a new beginning, a dramatic break with those values and traditions that had culminated in the Nazi catastrophe. As a German state, the republic continued national history, while as

---

[6] Compare D. Geyer, "Die DDR auf dem Weg zu einer eigenen historischen Identität? DDR-Geschichte und Geschichtswissenschaft zwischen Ost und West," in *DDR heute*, eds. G. Meyer and J. Schröder (Tübingen, 1988) and the essays in Konrad Jarausch, ed. *Zwischen Parteilichkeit und Professionalität. Bilanz der Geschichtswissenschaft der DDR* (Berlin, 1991).

a member of the European Community, a partner in the NATO alliance, and a successful democracy, it was a new Germany, freed from the burdens of the past.

Once again, a museum—or rather museum plans—will help us to see the shape of the official version of the past. Four years ago, Germans debated whether there should be a museum of German history in Berlin—a western equivalent of the Zeughaus exhibitions mentioned earlier. At the same time, plans were underway for a historical museum to be devoted to the Federal Republic, which was to be in Bonn and was not to be called a museum but rather a "House of History"— presumably for the same reasons that the West German constitution is called a "basic law" rather than a constitution. The coexistence of these two museums suggests the gap that continued to separate the Federal Republic and the German past, a past over which Bonn was prepared to act as a kind of executor: it was prepared to claim control over and sometimes to assume responsibility for German history, but was never quite willing to take full possession of it.[7]

The museum controversy also points toward that persistent sense of historical uncertainty that was part of the Federal Republic's political culture. West Germans never seemed to tire of writing and reading books about their identity problems. In 1980, for example, in a book significantly entitled "The German Neurosis," Peter Lerche wrote: "A people is able to act only when it can tell the story of its own past and identify with it. Germany today cannot do this, or can do it only with great difficulty. Their identity is thereby endangered." And in a work—again with a significant title, "The New Arrogance"— published in 1988, Arnulf Baring quoted with approval Dolf Sternberger's lament of 1949: "We don't know who we are.

---

[7] On the two museums, see *Protokoll der Anhörung zum Forum für Geschichte und Gegenwart* (Berlin, 1983–84) and the articles by Christoph Stölzl, Verena Tafel, and Hermann Schäfer in *Aus Politik und Zeitschichte* (8 January 1988).

That is the German question." Many observers seemed to assume this problem of identity came from Germany's unsettled relationship to their national past. "Germans of my generation," wrote Martin Walser, Jahrgang 1934, "cannot have an undisturbed relationship to reality—the very basis of our national reality is itself disrupted." And some, like Michael Stürmer, argued that only history could heal this disrupted relationship; as Stürmer put it in his inimitable—and untranslatable—prose: "in einem geschichtslosen Land die Zukunft gewinnt, wer die Erinnerung füllt, die Begriffe prägt und die Vergangenheit deutet"— "in a land without history the future belongs to those who fill memory, shape concepts, and determine the meaning of the past."[8]

Before going any further, perhaps we should pause for a moment and ask if the Federal Republic's identity problems may have been somewhat exaggerated. It seems to me that many of us—and I plead guilty to the charge—took the lamentations of Walser and Stürmer much too seriously. Now that the Federal Republic in its original form has come to an end, we can see that its identity was a good deal firmer than we might have thought. Whatever it might have been in 1949, by 1989 the Bonn republic was not "a land without history"—but rather a state that had created its own historical identity, an identity neither clearly tied nor clearly severed from the history that had preceded it, but firmly rooted in its own shared experiences, values, and institutions.

The Federal Republic was neither the historyless, anxious neurotic its intellectuals often described, nor the sleeping,

---

[8] Peter Lerche, ed., *Die Deutsche Neurose. Über die beschädigte Identität der Deutschen* (Frankfurt, 1980); Arnulf Baring, *Unser neuer Grössenwahn. Deutschland zwischen Ost und West* (Stuttgart, 1988), p. 33; Stürmer, "Geschichte in geschichtslosem Land," first published in the *Frankfurter Allgemeine Zeitung*, 25 April 1986, reprinted in *Historikerstreit. Die Dokumentation der Kontroverse um die Einzigartigkeit der nationalsozialistischen Judenvernichtung* (Munich, 1987), p. 36.

chauvinistic giant its enemies sometimes imagined. Rather it was a somewhat provincial, largely self-satisfied European state that happened to be tied by the force of history and the force of habit to a national policy about which most people had forgotten. It is, I think, in the light of this sense of themselves that we can best understand both the shallow enthusiasm and deep uneasiness with which many West Germans confronted unification. The federal government's absurd promises that unification was possible without much cost came not only from the politicians' fear of this uneasiness among their voters, but also from the simple fact that before 1989 no one in Bonn had thought much about the possibility that the GDR would cease to exist.

The degree to which the Federal Republic had established its distinctive historical identity was clear during what was one of the most fascinating public debates on history and identity in recent times: I am referring, of course, to the debate on the Hauptstadtfrage. The first remarkable thing about this debate was that it should have taken place at all. One might have thought the issue settled: by the historical precedent of 1871 to 1945, by forty years of rhetorical gestures and material subvention, and finally, by Article 2 of the Einigungsvertrag between the two German states. But the issue was by no means settled. All during the spring of 1991, the debate went on: it involved the narrowest of economic interests and the grandest of philosophical issues; it pulled to the surface regional rivalries and bad historical memories; it activated confessional tensions and personal ambitions; it cut across party lines and ideological divisions; most of all, it was a debate that was at least as much about the past as it was about the future.[9]

---

[9] The best place to follow this debate is in the pages of the *Frankfurter Allgemeine Zeitung*, which took a firmly pro-Berlin position. See the collection edited by Michael Mönninger, *Das neue Berlin* (Frankfurt and Leipzig, 1991). *Die Zeit* was much more ambivalent: see, for

The debate on the Hauptstadt was a wholesome exercise in public reflection. It is understandable why so many Germans were reluctant to move from Bonn, which did, after all, symbolize the best government they had ever had. It was also understandable why people were worried about how much this was going to cost them. It is not at all unfortunate that real estate seems to have been more important than Realpolitik. And it was understandable why the outcome was so close—a mere seventeen votes out of the over six hundred and fifty cast—an outcome that reflected the deeply divided feelings many people on both sides of the debate had about the question. In the end, however, the decision had to be for Berlin. To have decided otherwise would have been to deny history, most immediately the forty years in which the West looked on Berlin as its outpost of freedom and the East as its capital, but beyond that the years in which Berlin stood for so much that was ugly and repressive in German history, as well as for some of what was beautiful and progressive. Lewis Mumford says somewhere that great cities are all museums, instruments of memory that recall and recapture the past. There are few cities so drenched in history as Berlin—not merely in its old buildings and monuments, but also in its fragmentation, its odd empty spaces, and haphazard reconstruction of the past. These spatial breaks and architectural discontinuities are of particular historical interest because they represent the fragmentation, destruction, and reconstruction that is so central to the German experience in the modern era. One can only hope they do not all disappear under a monotonous shell of steel and glass—or even worse, under a leaden layer of what is thought to be postmodern wit.[10]

---

example, Theo Sommer's lead article, "Noch nicht daheim im deutschen Haus," *Die Zeit* (21 January 1991).

[10] We should look forward to a study of the move to Berlin comparable to R. Pommerin's *Von Berlin nach Bonn* (Cologne, 1989), which will trace the movement in the opposite direction.

The decision for Berlin, therefore, was—or should be—a decision to appropriate the German past. To say that, however, immediately raises the question, What past? A question which brings me directly to the issue promised by my title: What is the past that the new Germany will carry into its future?

Perhaps one should start by saying what this past is not: it surely is not the Prussian traditions recently evoked by the reburial of Frederick the Great in Potsdam. One does not know quite what to do with this desperate comedy except to say that there is as little of Frederick's Prussia left outside the coffin as there is of his mortal remains within. Nor can we take very seriously the current campaign to rebuild the Hohenzollern Schloss in Berlin. However much one might applaud the idea aesthetically—it was a fine building, destroyed by an irresponsible act of political vandalism—the project's implications are not very appealing. In any event, the campaign has little enough to do with the aesthetics of architecture and a good deal to do with settling old scores against the GDR. In that sense, the discussion of what should be torn down and what rebuilt in the eastern half of Berlin raises a much more serious issue: the need to come to terms with the immediate past, especially with the experience of national division and the legacy of the GDR.

There are two errors to be avoided from the outset. The first is to suppose that the two German states had separate histories, joined only at the beginning and end: Jürgen Habermas seems to have implied as much when he described his own relationship to the GDR as "unconnected" and declared that "their history was not our history." The second error is another version of the first; it is to suppose that there was only one legitimate German history after 1945, and this was the history of the Federal Republic—the history of the GDR was ungerman, foreign, a tragic but temporary break in the flow of national development. Both these views make it difficult to ask those questions about the past which are so vital for the future.[11]

The first of these questions concerns the origins of the new Germany: what were the immediate causes of the revolution of 1989? When one talks to people in East and West—in the "new" and "old" federal states—two alternative interpretations begin to emerge. One emphasizes the movement for reform within the GDR, a movement that picked up momentum after the local elections in May 1989—in which massive fraud was unmistakable—and culminated in the great Leipzig and Berlin demonstrations in the fall. According to this version, the movement towards a democratic, socialist East German state was thwarted by the intervention of the West, which used its financial resources and political influence to persuade a majority of easterners that their best chance was a rapid unification with the Federal Republic. An alternative interpretation of the events of 1989 emphasizes the massive westward emigration that began that summer as soon as it became clear that the GDR's eastern neighbors would not close their borders. According to this line of analysis, migration not only forced a series of concessions from the government but also left the West with no real alternative to unification—or, as some put it, the only choice was between a unification of the two states and national unification on West German soil. In this second version, the Federal Republic is not an aggressive seducer forcing its way on a naive and helpless East, but rather a reluctant groom who accepts his penniless bride because neither has a real choice in the matter.[12]

---

[11] Habermas in *Die Zeit* (3 May 1991). For a reaction from the former GDR, see Friedrich Dieckmann, "Unsere oder eine andere Geschichte?," *Berliner Tagesspiegel* (31 July 1991).

[12] For a powerful argument on the importance of emigration, see Norman Naimark, "'Ich will hier raus': Emigration and the Collapse of the German Democratic Republic," in *Eastern Europe in Revolution*, ed. Ivo Banac (Ithaca, N.Y. and London, 1992), pp. 72–95.

These two stories about what happened in 1989–90 offer two quite different perspectives from which to view the history of the GDR down to its eventual disappearance. Those who favor the first version tend to see the GDR as a potentially progressive country which might have been a true German social democracy. Tragically, this state fell into the hands of those who betrayed its ideals—these traitors, usually called "Stalinists," became increasingly alienated from their society as they retreated into a realm of private privilege and public paralysis. And then, just as the forces of democracy were coming to life again, they were overwhelmed by the false promises of the West. Those who favor the second version usually see a different GDR: for them, East Germany was not a potentially progressive state ruined by a small group of Stalinists, but rather a fatally and fundamentally flawed system, imposed on a reluctant people by Russian power and sustained by terror and repression. As soon as people had a chance to leave this system, a significant number took it; when they had a chance to vote in favor of unification with the West, an overwhelming majority did so. It is not hard to see how the outcome of this historical debate will be shaped both by what we learn about the past and by what happens in the future.[13]

Closely associated with these two views of the GDR are attitudes about the origins of Germany's initial division—an issue that is bound to reemerge now that the historical era begun by this division has come to an end. Despite the efforts of various "revisionist" historians, especially in the United States, the prevailing opinion in the West is that the division of Germany was imposed on the allies by Soviet intransigence, which broke the "grand alliance" and hardened the temporary division of occupation zones into two German states. Eastern

---

[13] On the future history of the GDR, see the essays in the collection edited by Jarausch, cited in note 6. Friedrich Dieckmann provides the insights of a critical "insider" in *Glockenläuten und offene Frage. Berichte und Diagnosen aus dem anderen Deutschland* (Frankfurt, 1991).

scholars have long taken a very different view of this process. They tend to take seriously various Soviet initiatives for a reunited German state. They regard the Stalin note of 1952, for example, as a serious offer through which a united Germany might, like Austria, have become a neutral nation. Once again, you can see how the question of responsibility for Germany's division affects not only how one views the subsequent history of the two German states, but also how one assesses their end

Just beyond the origins of the Cold War lies the problem of National Socialism, which has always been and will surely remain the most sensitive and troubling area of German history and historiography. As we have seen, the two German states approached this problem from different perspectives, but for both of them it was always enmeshed with their own rivalries. The concept of "fascism" in the East found its counterpart in the western term "totalitarianism"—both designed to convert the historical experience of Nazism into a propaganda weapon in the Cold War. Perhaps now that this war is over, it will be possible to reexamine how this dark chapter fits into German history after 1945. Once again, the future of this past will be shaped by contemporary developments: if the new state remains stable and secure, then it will be much easier to take possession of the Nazi past. The more loudly echoes of this past seem to sound in the present, the more troubling and unresolved it will continue to be, both for Germans and for their neighbors.

Of course beyond the Nazi years stretches the whole expanse of the German past. This too will take on a different shape with the creation of a new nation. Perhaps from the perspective of 1991, the first Reichsgründung will appear still more natural, Bismarck's Germany the only answer to the German question. But it is also possible that, once they have been freed from the political and ideological pressures of national division, German historians will be able to see more clearly the alternatives to unification in 1871 and its limitations in the years thereafter. And how will the creation of a successful democratic Germany affect our views of the national past? Will certain aspects of German history—the powerful participatory element in the Bismarckian Reich, for example—begin to seem more important as time goes on? And will the apparently irreversible drive towards greater European integration cause us to rethink our views on the German Sonderweg, that "special path" which many thought led from Germany's flawed modernization to the catastrophes of 1914 and 1933? Clearly this is not the time to try to answer these questions. But one thing is certain: no aspect of the German past will be left untouched by the new direction of Germany's future.[14]

Let me conclude these remarks in true Joycean manner, by returning to our point of departure, to *Ulysses*—and to what is perhaps the most famous quotation from the book, Stephan Dedalus's bitter comment that "History is a nightmare from which I am trying to awake." This lament appears towards the end of Chapter 2, where it is evoked by some anti-Semitic remarks of his headmaster, and thus it is thematically tied to the conversation in Barney Kiernan's pub that I quoted at the beginning. Stephan's view of the past is sometimes cited as though it were Joyce's own; this is, I think, a mistake. Joyce, to be sure, knew enough about history, and particularly about Irish history, to recognize its nightmarish side. But he also knew that history was not only the nightmare that haunts us, it was also the story of who we are—troubling and consoling, a source of conflict and cohesion, difficult to live with but impossible to live without.

---

[14] Two preliminary attempts to put the new nation in historical perspective: Christian Meier, "Die deutsche Einheit als Herausforderung," *Frankfurter Allgemeine Zeitung* (24 April 1990) and Jürgen Kocka, "Revolution und Nation 1989: Zur historischen Einordnung der gegenwärtigen Ereignisse," *Tel Aviver Jahrbuch für deutsche Geschichte* 19 (1990): pp. 479–99.

We should not, therefore, hope that in their new nation, Germans will awake from the nightmare of history, but rather that they will finally take possession of their past—all of their past, with its nightmares and its dreams, its hopes and failures, its continuities and fragmentations—and that they do so for the only convincing reason there is to appropriate the past: because it is, necessarily and unavoidably, theirs.

5

Paradigm Lost?
The "Sonderweg" Revisited[*]

Among the many things that national histories have in common is the conviction that each one of them is unique. Every nation has a history that reveals its exceptional character and fate; all national paths are special paths.

But while there is nothing unusual about German exceptionalism, it does have some distinctive characteristics. From the start, the founders of German national history defined their nation's exceptional character in terms of its relationship to the "west," whose politics, society, and culture they viewed with an unstable and varied mixture of admiration, envy, and dislike. Eighteenth-century thinkers like Herder contrasted the authenticity of German culture with the brittle cosmopolitanism of France; Heinrich Heine ironically chided his fellow countrymen for leaving to Britain the seas and to

---

[*]Published in Gunilla Budde, Sebastian Conrad, and Oliver Janz, eds., *Transnationale Geschichte: Themen, Tendenzen und Theorien (Jürgen Kocka zum 65. Geburtstag)* (Göttingen, 2006), pp. 150–60. I could not resist this title although I am not, alas, the first author to bring Milton and Kuhn together. In this essay, I shall use *paradigm* simply to mean an interpretive framework that encourages and coordinates empirical research.

France the land, while they themselves claimed dominion over "the airy realm of dreams." And, to cite one final example: at the end of the *Communist Manifesto*, Marx and Engels wrote that "Communists turn their attention chiefly to Germany" because here the bourgeois revolution that had taken place earlier in the west would occur under more advanced conditions, thereby setting off a revolutionary movement in Europe as a whole. The German Sonderweg, therefore, was always inseparable from a recognition of Germany's relative "backwardness," although Germans differed about whether this backwardness was a source of exceptional virtue, weakness, or opportunity.[1]

In the late nineteenth and early twentieth centuries, German exceptionalism became more ideologically active and politically focused as it was deployed in defense of the imperial status quo, a development that culminated during the First World War when the nation's intellectuals rallied to defend German *Kultur* against the aggressive superficiality of western civilization. At the same time that the conservative version of the Sonderweg was given its most strident formulation by writers like Werner Sombart and Thomas Mann, we can find many of the most important elements of a competing, highly critical version of German exceptionalism in books such as Thorstein Veblen's *Imperial Germany and the Industrial Revolution*, which was first published in 1915. Like most of Veblen's work, this is an undisciplined, eccentrically brilliant book, combining wildly implausible assertions with shrewd and compelling analysis. Veblen's key insight—which would become a persistent feature of the critical Sonderweg—was to define German exceptionalism not simply as a product of backwardness but as a problematic mixture of backwardness and modernity. Germany's flawed, incomplete process of modernization gave it access to the powerful forces created by industrialism but without the attendant liberalization that had occurred in Britain.

---

[1] See B. Faulenbach, *Ideologie des deutschen Weges* (München, 1980).

In an early, generally quite positive review, the American historian Guy Stanton Ford provided this concise statement of the question at the core of Veblen's book: "What is the result when the modern economic order based on technological methods is amalgamated with a social and political order still essentially medieval?"[2] For Veblen in 1915, the "result" was the war between German feudal militarism and British liberal individualism then being waged on Europe's battlefields. After 1945, the "result" seemed to be Nazi tyranny and racial murder, which gave the problem of German exceptionalism a new and terrible significance and put its origins and character at the core of what came to be known as "the German question."

National Socialism gave the concept of German exceptionalism its most uncompromisingly toxic formulation. But seen from the outside, the Nazi regime revealed the pathological implications of Germany's deviance from the West. In 1935, for example, Helmuth Plessner, who had been forced into exile in the Netherlands, published *Schicksal deutschen Geistes im Ausgang seiner bürgerlichen Epoche*, a precocious analysis of Germany as a "verspätete Nation." In 1943, two influential works appeared in the United States: Alexander Gerschenkron's *Bread and Democracy in Germany* (University of California Press) and Hans Rosenberg's "Political and Social Consequences of the Great Depression of 1873–1896" (*Economic History Review*, XIII, p. 58–73). The perspectives advanced in these works were further developed after the war: in 1952, for instance, Hajo Holborn published his seminal essay on "Der deutsche Idealismus in sozial-geschichtlicher Beleuchtung" (*HZ*, CLXXIV, 359–84), which subjected the conventional core of German cultural identity to a critical analysis; Hans Rosenberg's *Bureaucracy, Aristocracy, and Autocracy: The Prussian Experience, 1660–1815* (Cambridge, MA, 1958) provided a more highly charged critique of the apolitical

---

[2] *American Historical Review*, 21 (1916), pp. 801–2.

Prussian civil service and the progressive reforms of the early nineteenth century. Both Holborn and Rosenberg, émigrés teaching in the United States, implicitly compared the German case to the normative evolution of western institutions and values.[3]

Two works published in the early 1960s mark a significant stage in the maturation of the Sonderweg paradigm, as well as its reimportation into Germany. Fritz Fischer's monumental *Griff nach der Weltmacht* (Düsseldorf, 1961) did more than any other book to establish the Sonderweg in the Bundesrepublik. The implications of Fischer's argument, and the chief source of its immediate notoriety and lasting influence, went far beyond his ostensible subject, which was the evolution of German war aims between 1914 and 1918. In the first place, Fischer brought back to life the old charge that Germany was responsible for causing the war. Second, he maintained that Germany's decision for war was not the result of individual miscalculation or geopolitical disadvantage but rather arose from the desperate necessity of escaping domestic political conflicts. Finally and most importantly, he emphasized the continuity between the Kaiserreich and National Socialism: Germany's problems did not start in 1914 or 1918 or 1933, they were deeply rooted in the unresolved tensions of the nineteenth century. This continuity was personified by Chancellor Bethmann Hollweg, whom Fischer transformed from a tragic victim of circumstance into an eager advocate of national expansion, an important link in the unbroken chain of aggressors that connected Bismarck to Hitler. This thesis, developed by Fischer himself and expanded upon by his students and admirers, became one of the Sonderweg's most important themes, the source of scores of books and articles

---

[3] See H. Lehmann and J. Sheehan eds., *An Interrupted Past: German Speaking Refugee Historians in the United States after 1933* (Cambridge, 1991).

and of the most intense historiographical controversies of the postwar era.[4]

Although very different from Fischer in style, approach, and method, Ralf Dahrendorf's *Gesellschaft und Demokratie in Deutschland* (München, 1965) was based on a similar view of the German past. Fischer's strength was the overwhelming depth of his research, Dahrendorf's, the breadth of his analysis, which included historical developments and contemporary institutions, politics and culture, private habits and public values. More explicitly than Fischer, Dahrendorf defined Germany's problems in terms of what it lacked: a socially transformative industrial revolution, a strong liberal movement, a cohesive modernizing elite, and a willingness to accept the progressive possibilities of conflict. The Second World War, he argued, had finally provided the revolutionary changes Germany needed, but disturbing remnants of the old order remained to threaten the shallow roots of liberal democracy.

In the 1970s, the critical Sonderweg became the dominant paradigm for modern German historiography. Hans-Ulrich Wehler's *Das deutsche Kaiserreich*, based on lectures given in the late sixties and published in 1973, was its sharpest, most decisive formulation, the *locus classicus* for both the Sonderweg's advocates and critics. The series *Kritische Studien zur Geschichtswissenschaft*, which began to appear in 1972, published a series of monographs and collected essays informed by the paradigm, as was the journal *Geschichte und Gesellschaft*, which was founded by Wehler and several of his colleagues in 1975. Wehler also edited a series (beginning in 1971 and eventually including nine volumes) entitled *Deutsche Historiker*, which established the Sonderweg's historiographical lineage with accounts of often-neglected outsiders and critics. Wehler's

---

[4] For a guide to the Fischer debate, see H. Böhme, "'Primat' und 'Paradigmata,'" in Lehmann ed., *Historikerkontroversen* (Göttingen, 2000), pp. 89–139.

essay "Geschichtswissenschaft heute," published in *Stichworte zur "Geistigen Situation der Zeit,"* edited by Jürgen Habermas (Frankfurt, 1979) not only summarized the Sonderweg position but also claimed for it a historiographical primacy. In Wehler's account the Sonderweg was "Geschichtswissenschaft heute."

It would be a mistake to underestimate the diversity among the Sonderweg's many adherents, but, to use Wittgenstein's indispensable metaphor, they formed a historiographical "family" that shared an overlapping set of values, assumptions, and commitments. Five characteristics of this historiographical family help us to understand its place within the Federal Republic's political culture and to explain its persistent power and appeal.

1. The Sonderweg offered a powerful and compelling answer to the central problem of German national history: how was Nazism possible? But it told the national story from an international perspective, not only because of its inherently comparative nature (which was no less potent because it was often implicit), but also because it was formed within the dense network of trans-Atlantic relationships that had been woven by the émigrés and then sustained by scholarly exchanges in both directions. Among the most powerful intellectual sources for the paradigm were scholars like Holborn and Rosenberg, whose students and followers, both German and American, became leading representatives of Sonderweg scholarship. The Sonderweg was, therefore, an element in that connection to the west that pervaded every aspect of politics and culture in the Bundesrepublik.

2. The Sonderweg was a generational phenomenon. Although its founding fathers, including émigrés like Holborn and Rosenberg and the key German figure, Fritz Fischer, were born in the first decade of the twentieth century, the paradigm was consolidated and spread by their scholarly progeny, that is, scholars born in the 1930s. The members of this generation

were old enough to have witnessed Nazism; some had been active on the edges of the movement, usually as members of the Hitler Youth. But they were young enough to have escaped direct involvement with its crimes. This was also the first generation of postwar exchange students, many of whom were powerfully influenced by their first contacts with Britain or America. And this generation was, of course, the chief beneficiary of the expansion of German higher education in the 1960s, which created new universities, new chairs, and new opportunities. One reason for the Sonderweg's persistence was simply that its adherents entered academic life at the most favorable possible moment and acquired positions that they would retain for the next thirty years.

3. The Sonderweg was a liberal perspective—that is, liberal in the Anglo-American sense, which became the model for many of the young German scholars who had spent time in the United States or Britain. As liberals, and in contrast to Marxists and conservatives, they endorsed the central institutions of the modern world, not without criticism, but as at least potentially progressive. Because modernity was healthy, its belatedness, incompleteness, or insufficiency were necessarily pathological. In the west German context, this commitment to liberalism meant accepting—again, not uncritically—the three pillars on which the Federal Republic rested: welfare capitalism, parliamentary democracy, and an alliance with the west, especially the United States.

4. The Sonderweg scholars were liberal but, like most German liberals in the decades after 1945, they were concerned that liberal institutions and values might not be firmly rooted enough to withstand future crises and temptations. From this concern came the civic project that gave the Sonderweg its polemical energy and political direction: the pressing need to free the Bundesrepublik from those residues from the past that inhibited the growth of an authentic democratic culture and society. This was to be done by giving Germans a critical

perspective on their past, a new kind of national history that could inform both political debate and scholarly controversy— indeed the distinction between the two was often hard to see.

5. As important as these political and generational factors surely were, they should not distract us from what I believe was the most important reason for the Sonderweg's appeal: it suggested a vitally interesting scholarly agenda, a series of significant new problems on which scholars could do useful empirical research. Much of this research contributed to what Georg Iggers called "the social history of politics," including studies of political parties and movements, of social, political, and cultural elites, of economic organizations and cultural institutions, and of the domestic origins and implications of foreign policy. The Sonderweg narrative was filled with absences, failures, and missed opportunities. Sonderweg scholarship often clustered around issues where modernity and backwardness seemed interwoven: "revolutions from above," the "democratization" of the aristocracy, the "feudalization" of the middle classes, and "organized" capitalism. The Sonderweg was flexible enough to embrace a variety of problems, yet coherent enough to enable scholars to feel that their work fit within a large framework. It offered scope for originality without imposing excessive restrictions or conformity. Above all, therefore, the Sonderweg's success as an approach to German history is reflected in the remarkable quantity and quality of the scholarship it inspired.

From the beginning, the Sonderweg had a provocative style and a polemical edge, which were already apparent in the work of Eckart Kehr, who was adopted as the paradigm's heroic pioneer, as well as in that of its founding fathers like Fischer and Rosenberg. The advocates of the critical Sonderweg defined their approach to German history in opposition to what they saw as the political, methodological, and substantive failings of the historiographical establishment: they were liberals rather than conservatives, critics rather than apologists, openly political rather than supposedly neutral; the history they wrote was theoretically informed rather than mere narrative, it had to do with social groups and political movements rather than ideas or great men, it sought to explain continuities and structures rather than unique events or individuals. Behind this opposition were, to be sure, deep similarities between the advocates of the Sonderweg and the historiographical establishment, similarities that gave these their shape and significance: both sides accepted the idea of German exceptionalism; both worked within national categories, indeed both had an essentially Prussocentric, kleindeutsch definition of German history; even though they had quite different ideas about politics, both assumed the primacy of political questions; and finally, both saw history as an essential pedagogical instrument in building the kind of nation they wanted. In that sense, there was a certain amount of truth in Thomas Nipperdey's otherwise unfair description of Wehler as "Treitschke redivivus."[5]

Born from the need to provide an alternative to the failures of conventional history, the Sonderweg was sustained by a series of controversies that dominated German historical writing for two decades. The advocates of the Sonderweg were criticized for being one-sided, deterministic, and excessively ideological. Scholars of international relations objected, not surprisingly, to the apparent marginalization of their subject, which was subordinated to the "Primat der Innenpolitik." Rather less predictably, scholars interested in Alltagsgeschichte found themselves in a sharp polemic over the role of politics in social history. Margaret Anderson and Kenneth Barkin pointed out that the Sonderweg's dualistic view of the nineteenth century left no room for political Catholicism, which did not easily fit within a struggle between modernity

---

[5] Nipperdey, "Wehlers Kaiserreich: Eine kritische Auseinandersetzung," *Geschichte und Gesellschaft* 1 (1975): pp. 539–60.

and backwardness. But perhaps the most influential critique of the Sonderweg came from a group of British scholars who challenged the very foundation of its interpretative structure: David Blackbourn and Geoff Eley argued that the Sonderweg rested on an idealized and unrealistic image of the "West" and an overly rigid, normative concept of modernization. Blackbourn and Eley's criticisms triggered a series of polemical exchanges, the echoes of which continue to be heard, albeit more faintly, in the scholarly literature. The Sonderweg's critics revealed a number of conceptual weaknesses, empirical problems, and logical flaws, but they implicitly acknowledged the Sonderweg's persistent significance, its capacity to remain the center of scholarly attention and to set the terms of historiographical debates.[6]

In practice, the defenders of the Sonderweg were always more flexible and receptive to criticism than they sometimes appeared to their opponents. Over time, the contours of the paradigm changed—the weakness of the German Bürgertum, for instance, became less important, the peculiarities of the German political system, more so. The analysis of the German past in Wehler's *Gesellschaftsgeschichte* is very different from the one in *Das deutsche Kaiserreich*; Jürgen Kocka's defense of the paradigm has become progressively more qualified and nuanced.[7] Nevertheless, the paradigm has displayed a remarkable persistence; despite the frequent appearance of

---

[6] For a guide to these controversies, see C. Lorenz, "Beyond Good and Evil? The German Empire of 1871 and Modern German Historiography," *Journal of Contemporary History*, 30 (1995): pp. 729–67.

[7] Kocka, "German History before Hitler: The Debate on the German Sonderweg," *Journal of Contemporary History*, 23 (1988): pp. 3–16; "Nach dem Ende des Sonderwegs. Zur Tragfähigkeit eines Konzepts," in: Arnd Bauerkämper et al eds., *Doppelte Zeitgeschichte* (Bonn, 1998), pp. 364–75.

obituaries, it remains very much alive if no longer quite as robust as it once was.

In history, unlike the natural and some of the social sciences, controversies rarely end with the clear victory of one side or the other; in liberal societies, historians lack the institutional power and intellectual authority to silence their opponents. Competing historiographical paradigms, therefore, are usually displaced rather than disproved. To some degree at least, this happened to the Sonderweg after 1989, when the collapse of the GDR and the creation of a new German state changed Germany's future and therefore its past. Once the postwar era came to an end and a treasure trove of new documents became available, the center of scholarly concerns shifted away from the nineteenth century; continuities between the Kaiserreich and Nazism became less interesting than comparisons between the two German dictatorships. Germans now had yet another past to master.

Although the fall of the GDR generated a number of new historical issues and opportunities, it did not create a new paradigm for German historiography. Instead, surveying the situation fifteen years later, one is struck by the rich variety of subjects that are attracting important new research. Some of them, such as the new interest in the social history of war and military institutions or the development of nationalism, clearly could fit within the Sonderweg. Others, such as the variety of works on the Bürgertum, deepen and broaden our understanding of what had always been a key element in the paradigm. Some of the most important new research opens up areas that the Sonderweg had ignored or undervalued: the history of religion, for instance, and the role of the Mittelstaaten and regions. A couple of decades after its arrival in British, French, and American historiography, gender has become an important historical category in Germany. Cultural history in all its many forms has also become increasingly popular. Finally, many more German historians now take on the challenging task of writing explicit, sustained comparative histories of movements, social groups, or institutions.

In addition to its fecund diversity, the other striking characteristic of German historiography in 2005 is the remarkable number of programmatic statements about, and critical analyses of, scholarly trends. Even to list these would exhaust the supply of words I have been assigned for this essay, so I shall confine myself to two examples:

Konrad Jarausch, in a series of essays and in a book co-authored with Michael Geyer, has recently urged historians to abandon not only the Sonderweg but all "master narratives," and thus recapture the past's variety and fragmentation. In Jarausch's view, German history loses is unity, continuity, and particularity. Far from suffering from a lack of modernization, Germany was "a site of an unusual accumulation of some general problems of modernity;" although, like the defenders of a Sonderweg, he acknowledges that these problems arose in a "somewhat traditional society" and thus "produced more backlash than elsewhere."[8] Like Jarausch and Geyer, Jürgen Osterhammel wants to move beyond the usual narratives, but his proposal is to extend rather than shatter the conventional picture of the German past. As the title of his collected essays suggests, Osterhammel seeks a history "jenseits des Nationalstaats," sensitive to global connections and comparisons. The result would not be to abandon the nation as a historiographical category but rather a greater awareness of its place in a network of relationships, both global and local.[9]

---

[8] Jarausch and Geyer, *Shattered Past* (Princeton, 2003), pp. 368–69. See also Jarausch and M. Sabrow eds., *Die historische Meistererzählung. Deutungslinien der deutschen Nationalgeschichte nach 1945* (Göttingen, 2002).

[9] Osterhammel, *Geschichtswissenschaft jenseits des Nationalstaaats. Studien zu Beziehungsgeschichte und Zivilisationsvergleich* (Göttingen, 2001). See also H. W. Smith's thoughtful analysis of Osterhammel, "For a

The appearance of so many programmatic statements like those by Jarausch, Geyer, and Osterhammel is, I think, a symptom of the unsettled state of the discipline, of the passing of one paradigm and, perhaps, of the gradual emergence of its successor.

Is the Sonderweg as exhausted as some proclaim or does it remain the best way to explain some central problems of German history? Is there a new paradigm on the horizon, a new master narrative of the German past or a fusion of German and European, even global history? It would be rash to propose answers to these questions. As Dieter Langewiesche has recently reminded us, "historians are only qualified to look backwards. As experts, they are fundamentally unable to offer prognoses."[10] Instead of answers about the future of German historiography, let me suggest some questions that might help us think about it. To do so, I shall return to the five sources of the Sonderweg's influence that I mentioned earlier.

1. The first question to be posed is about the future of national history. How will the unification of 1991, the creation and expansion of the European Union, and the weakening of trans-Atlantic ties affect the way Germans think about their past? At the moment, there seems to be little sign of a nationalist revival in German history. Might there instead be a new kind of postnational history, a European orientation that would replace the Atlantic one, the historiographical equivalent of NATO's eclipse by an EU security force?

2. The generation of scholars most closely associated with the Sonderweg has now retired; most of them are still highly

---

Differently Centered Central European History," *Central European History* 37 (2004): pp. 115–36.

[10] Langewiesche, "Postmoderne als Ende der 'Moderne'?" in W. Pyta and L. Richter, eds., *Gestaltungskraft des Politischen* (Berlin,

productive, but their institutional influence has clearly declined. What are the experiences that have marked the current generation of historians? And how will the current problems of German universities affect the forms and substance of historical scholarship? Will this, as one might expect, make the creation of a new dominant paradigm more difficult?

3. The Sonderweg rested on twin commitments to the normative power of modernity and to the usefulness of modernization as an explanatory concept. Will these commitments be eroded by contemporary problems? How, for instance, will the crises of welfare capitalism, German-American relations, and ethnic diversity shape the politics of German history and the history of German politics?

4. Just as a commitment to modernity was central to the Sonderweg's interpretation of the German past, so a faith in the value of historical science and in the possibility of historical truth helped to sustain their engagement in a Habermasean public sphere. Has this faith been eroded by a rising tide of postmodern skepticism? And even if, as there is good reason to believe, postmodernism is a passing fad, will historians continue to play a prominent role in Germany's public discourse or will they—as has happened in the United States, for example—be elbowed aside by economists and other social scientists?

5. Finally, what empirical problems will engage historians in the decades ahead? Will the apparent fragmentation of historical interests continue, or will historians find another framework for their work which can, like the Sonderweg, can shape research by posing questions to be addressed? Will Konrad Jarausch's "plurale, interpendente Narrative" or Osterhammel's postnational perspective provide fertile soil for scholarly research? We have found that living with a paradigm can be difficult; will we discover that living without one is harder still?

Of these five sets of questions, the last seems to me to be by far the most important. Thomas Kuhn once remarked that the development of science is determined by what scientists do rather by what they say they are going to do—that is, by their research rather than by their reflections on its meaning and direction. The same thing is true of historiography. We are, I think, always better advised to pay attention to the research that absorbs historians' time and energy, rather than to their statements about what they should, or might, or want to do. The future of German historiography will not be decided by programmatic pronouncements, no matter how eloquent or plausible they may be. History is a discipline that best expresses itself in practice, not theory; the possibilities of a historical paradigm are measured by how much it can help us learn interesting and significant things about the past. Historiographical programs are like maps, which may be useful to guide our explorations, but should never be mistaken for the journey itself.

Part II

6

Three Generations of German *Gelehrtenpolitik**

In 1922, the *Historische Zeitschrift* published an article by its editor, Friedrich Meinecke, entitled "Drei Generationen deutscher Gelehrtenpolitik."[1] *Gelehrtenpolitik* is one of those words that looks easy to translate until one tries to do it: for our purposes, we can render it as "the relationship of scholars to politics." The occasion for Meinecke's essay was the nearly simultaneous appearance of three books: the collected critical essays of Friedrich Theodor Vischer (1807–1887), a philosopher and historian of art, and the political writings of Gustav von Schmoller (1838–1917), an important economic historian and a founder of the Verein für Sozialpolitik, and of Max Weber (1864–1920), the great social theorist. Using these

---

*Originally published in the *Bulletin of the German Historical Institute Washington, D.C.* 39 (Fall 2006): pp. 39–43, as a comment on Gerhard A. Ritter's paper "German Emigré Historians Between Two Worlds" that appeared in the same issue of the *Bulletin*.
[1] That this essay was the subject of Felix Gilbert's contribution to the festschrift for Hajo Holborn links it even more closely to the subject of Gerhard Ritter's paper "Political Power and Academic Responsibility: Reflections on Friedrich Meinecke's *Drei Generationen deutscher Gelehrtenpolitik*," in *The Responsibility of Power: Historical Essays in Honor of Hajo Holborn*, eds. Leonard Krieger and Fritz Stern (Garden City, 1967), pp. 402–15.

three works as his point of departure, Meinecke traced the shift from idealism to empiricism to realism, from Vischer's slow reconciliation with a Prussian-dominated Germany to Schmoller's unquestioning acceptance of the Kaiserreich to Weber's critical and increasingly pessimistic nationalism. *Gelehrtenpolitik*, Meinecke wrote, can surely be found outside of Germany, but nowhere else is it so tightly wound up with decisive moments in national history.[2]

Gerhard Ritter's richly informative and deeply moving paper also presents us with three generations of German scholars: first, there is Meinecke's generation—he was born in 1862, two years before Weber, although he lived thirty four years longer, until 1954; next, the generation of his protégés—born around the turn of the last century; and, finally, there is Professor Ritter's own generation, that is the generation that was born at the end of the Weimar Republic, experienced Nazism as children and adolescents, and then came of age in the years after 1945. Following Meinecke's model, I want to reflect on each of these generations and suggest what they can tell us about the changing character of German *Gelehrtenpolitik* in the 20th century.

I begin with Meinecke himself. Meinecke's discussion of Weber in his 1922 essay clearly had an autobiographical element. After all, Weber belonged to his own generation: both men were marked intellectually by what Meinecke once called a new appreciation for the fragmentary quality of life and politically by a growing concern for political problems created by the Kaiser's erratic personality and the nation's unresolved social conflicts.[3] Meinecke set these experiences against both Vischer's idealism and the greater confidence—at once

[3] For Meinecke's own description of his generation's political and intellectual orientation, see his *Erlebtes*, reprinted in *Werke*, vol. 8 (Stuttgart, 1969), p. 100.

philosophical and political—that characterized Schmoller's approach to scholarship and politics. Just as the centerpiece of the section on Vischer is his reconciliation with Bismarck's Germany, so the center of the section on Weber is the disruptive power of war, military defeat, and political revolution.

From our perspective, however, the most striking characteristic of Meinecke's life is not disruption but connection. Part of this is simply chronological, a connection of past and present, the traditional and the modern: born four years before the battle of Königgrätz into what was a very old–fashioned social milieu, he died nine years after the battle of Berlin, in a world shaped by total war and shadowed by the danger of nuclear cataclysm. Intellectually, Meinecke bridged the evolution of German historiography from Ranke—whose funeral he attended as a student—and Droysen, through Nietzsche and Dilthey, to Weber and Troeltsch. Meinecke's politics also stretched across a broad span of historical experience: he lived in the Prussian monarchy, the German empire, republic, dictatorship, and finally in occupied and divided Berlin. Nevertheless, he remained, in many ways, a liberal nationalist—small *l*, small *n*—whose values and attitudes were shaped by the patriotic Protestant Bildungsbürgertum to which he belonged. From his early biography of the military reformer Hermann von Boyen to the core chapters in his magisterial *Vom Weltbürgertum zum Nationalstaat*, Meinecke was drawn to the era of Prussian reforms and national revival in the early nineteenth century— the critical chapter in liberal nationalism's grand narrative of German history. He remained a monarchist at heart, but he became, as Professor Ritter shows us, a republican by conviction, which certainly was an important reason why he attracted the progressive young men and women who became his protégés. This political flexibility, combined with personal integrity, a deeply rooted tolerance, and remarkable generosity of spirit, made him—as Felix Gilbert wrote—"one of the very few whose work and voice helped to join present and future with the better traditions of German scholarship."[4]

These same qualities also make Meinecke a tragic figure, a representative of a lost Germany, one of those decent, well–meaning men who were unable to prevent or even fully to understand their nation's catastrophic course. There is something heroic about Meinecke's book on the German catastrophe, written under difficult circumstances in the deep winter of his own and his nation's life. But it is also, I think, a sad and disappointing book.[5]

Meinecke arrived in Berlin in 1914 to take up the most important chair in German history, but for obvious reasons his impact on the next scholarly generation was delayed by the war. Among his protégés, only Dietrich Gerhard was old enough to serve. The rest—born in the first years of the twentieth century—experienced the war vicariously, through newspapers and what they heard from their older contemporaries. In his remarkable autobiography, Sebastian Haffner (born in 1907) has left us a vivid picture of what a wartime boyhood was like. Meinecke's protégés had, of course, scholarly temperaments. They were certainly committed to the Republic and attracted by the vibrant culture of Weimar Berlin, but they also did what young historians must do, spending more time in archives and libraries than in night clubs and cabarets. I am eager to read the letters Gerhard Ritter has assembled, but the autobiographical material I have seen is remarkably restrained about their emotional lives—for example, Felix Gilbert's memoir, *A European Past*, is a wonderful book in many ways, but it is also extraordinarily—one might say frustratingly—discreet. It is not easy to imagine these serious young scholars in the Weimar

---

[4] Gilbert, *History: Choice and Commitment* (Cambridge, MA, 1977), pp. 67–68.

[5] *Die deutsche Katastrophe* was written in the immediate aftermath of the war. It is reprinted in Meinecke's *Werke*, vol. 8, pp. 323–447.

scene described, for example, by Klaus Mann (born 1906) in his memoirs.[6]

These scholars were, as Professor Ritter shows us, drawn to Meinecke not simply because of his political sympathies but also—perhaps mainly—because of his reputation as an innovative historian, someone who was not tied to the narrow forms of political history practiced by the neo–Rankean establishment. It is striking how much of their early work— Gilbert on Droysen, Rosenberg on Haym—remained within the liberal national tradition, even if its political tone was sharper and more critical. From the start, however, Meinecke's protégés were a diverse group, differing from one another in scholarly interests and in temperament. To quote Gilbert once again: Meinecke "was a great teacher because he urged his students to find their own way, the way most appropriate to their personality." His students, Gilbert went on, "have worked in the most varied areas of history: political, social, institutional, intellectual. It was Meinecke's concern for their finding in history both a strict discipline and creative expression that brought students close to him and generated veneration for him, even if in their life and work they went on different roads."[7]

This diversity increased during the protégés' time in the United States: Dietrich Gerhard, as Ritter has shown us, was intellectually closer to Otto Hintze than to Meinecke. Hans Rosenberg quickly abandoned intellectual biography, first for economic history, then for a politically shaped social history. In some ways, Holborn and Gilbert stayed closer to their teacher, in their continued concern for political ideas and the history of historiography. But they too moved far away from

---

[6] As Michael Wildt has shown, members of this generation—from a very different milieu than Meinecke's students—played key roles in Nazism's terror apparatus: *Generation des Unbedingten* (Hamburg, 2003).

[7] Gilbert, *History*, p. 87.

the grand intellectual history that represented Meinecke's most significant work.

But despite the differences among them, we should not lose sight of two important things that Meinecke's protégés shared. First, all of them were attracted by, and became part of, the American historical profession, absorbing many of its values, reading widely in its literature, and contributing to its common life. Gerhard and Gilbert both published important works on American history. Holborn became president of the American Historical Association. And Rosenberg's scholarly developpment after 1933 was deeply influenced by his engagement with American contributions to history and the social sciences.[8]

And yet, while all four scholars flourished—not, it should be noted, without varying degrees of difficulty and at considerable cost—in their adopted homeland, all of them remained German. This is the second important thing they had in common: All of them returned to Germany—Rosenberg and Gerhard to spend the last years of their lives. After 1945, all of them resumed their ties to Meinecke and to other German friends. All of them had strong institutional connections to postwar German academic life. In the moving remarks he gave in 1977, on the occasion of being given an honorary degree at Bielefeld, Hans Rosenberg offered his listeners this description of himself: "Before you," he said, "stands an engaged historian, a non–Marxist, liberal– democratic, cosmopolitan German-American historian from the generation of 1904."[9] In this self-definition, the three most important words are German, American, and historian.

---

[8] On the role of the émigrés in the United States, see *An Interrupted Past: German-Speaking Refugee Historians in the United States after 1933*, eds. Hartmut Lehmann and James J. Sheehan (Cambridge, 1991).
[9] "Rückblick auf ein Historikerleben zwischen zwei Kulturen," in *Machteliten und Wirtschaftskonjunkturen: Studien zur neueren_deutschen Sozial—und Wirtschaftsgeschichte* (Göttingen, 1978), p. 12.

Because they were all German *and* American historians, Meinecke's protégés served as living links between the world they had been forced to leave and the new one in which they found a place. This was their great contribution to the generation of German historians who began their careers in the wreckage of the postwar world. What Gilbert said about Meinecke was even more powerfully and significantly true of these émigrés: their work and characters "helped to join present and future with the better traditions of German scholarship." And equally important, they helped to join the postwar generation to the scholarly world outside of Germany, and especially to Britain and the United States. As teachers, mentors, colleagues, and friends, the émigrés enriched both their new homes and their old, weaving connections that transformed Americans' understanding of Germany and Germans' understanding of America. They were, therefore, one thread—among many others—from which the political and cultural fabric of transatlantic relationships was woven. Professor Ritter, I know, would agree that postwar German historiography is impossible to imagine without them.

A final word about generations. In his classic essay on the concept of generation, first published in 1928, Karl Mannheim wrote: "Were it not for the existence of social interaction between human beings—were there no definable social structure, no history based on a particular sort of continuity, the generation would not exist as a social phenomenon; there would be merely birth, ageing and death."[10]

We historians are drawn to the concept of generation precisely because it helps us to understand both separation and connection, that constant interplay of continuities and changes that gives history its peculiar form and endless fascination. In

---

[10] "The Problem of Generations," reprinted in *From Karl Mannheim*, Kurt Wolff ed., 2nd ed. (New Brunswick, 1993), p. 366.

the three generations of German historians who have been our subject this evening, we can see the formative power of distinctive historical experiences: for Meinecke, the crisis and collapse of Bismarck's Reich; for his protégés, the failure of democracy and the anguish and opportunities of exile; and for the first postwar generation, the shadow of Nazism and the challenge of building a new democratic state. And yet spanning these great historical ruptures were powerful lines of continuity—lines of continuity woven from personal ties and also from a shared commitment to the scholar's calling. These lines of continuity unite our three very different generations and join them to the long and complex genealogy of German *Gelehrtenpolitik*.

We are all indebted to Gerhard Ritter for his splendid account of Meinecke and his protégés, in which he so eloquently portrayed the bonds of friendship and scholarly commitment that connect these generations to one another— and to many of us.

7

The Primacy of Domestic Politics:
Eckart Kehr's Essays on
Modern German History[*]

Eckart Kehr was born in 1902 and thus belonged to that generation of Germans whose youth was darkened by war, defeat, and social upheaval. In contrast to many historians in the 1920's, who sought refuge from these vicissitudes in an idealized past or a mythical future, Kehr turned to German history in order to uncover the roots of the present's discontents. The nature of this enterprise, which was as unfashionable as it was necessary, together with Kehr's disrespect for the political and methodological sensibilities of the professional establishment, prevented him from achieving the academic success his talents so clearly deserved. Nevertheless, the magnitude of these talents and the enormous

[*]A review essay of *Der Primat der Innenpolitik: Gesammelte Aufsätze zur preussisch-deutschen Sozialgeschichte im 19. und 20. Jahrhundert*, edited with an introduction by Hans-Ulrich Wehler; Foreword by Hans Herzfeld (Berlin, 1965). Published in *Central European History*, 1, no. 2 (June 1968): pp. 166–74. In 1977, the University of California Press published an English edition of ten of Kehr's essays, edited by Gordon Craig: *Economic Interest, Militarism, and Foreign Policy: Essays on German History*.

energy with which he applied them enabled Kehr to accomplish an extraordinary amount in his tragically brief lifetime. When he died in 1933 at the age of thirty-one, he left a lasting contribution to historical scholarship: a monograph on the domestic origins of naval expansion in the 1890's, *Schlachtflottenbau und Parteipolitik*, which remains one of the half-dozen best books on Wilhelmian Germany; a manuscript on "Economics and Politics in the Prussian Reform Era," which apparently has been lost; two volumes of documents on the reformers' financial policies, which have not yet been published; and a number of essays and articles. In *Der Primat der Innenpolitik*, Hans-Ulrich Wehler has collected these short pieces and has prefaced them with a sensitive and perceptive introduction which gives the available biographical information on Kehr and places him within the context of twentieth-century German historiography.

Kehr's approach to German history was shaped by two convictions. First, he believed that the difficulties Germany faced in the postwar world could not be explained by the influence of "foreign" ideas or the machinations of enemies at home and abroad, but had to be understood in terms of structural flaws in prewar German society. His research on the bureaucracy, the army, the diplomatic isolation of the empire, and the sources of German imperialism was engendered by his desire to comprehend and to alleviate contemporary problems. Second, Kehr was convinced that the modes of analysis employed by the historical establishment in Germany not only precluded a true understanding of the past but also perpetuated myths which had unhealthy political consequences. The cutting edge of Kehr's attack on the establishment was always both methodological and ideological since in his view the two were essentially inseparable. Thus the biographical emphasis of traditional historiography came from "a peculiar mixture of liberal individualism and subservience to a strong man" (p. 71). The unpopularity of social history in Germany was part of the propertied classes' fear of social unrest and the "grotesque identification of social history with socialist history" (p. 259). Similarly, Ideengeschichte was an escape from reality for those members of a "spiritually leaderless Bürgertum" who could neither bow to the Machtstaat nor join its critics on the left (p. 261). Kehr's own work must be seen in the light of his conscious rejection of these historical fashions, fashions he took to be both methodologically naive and politically regressive.[1]

Kehr devoted himself to the study of two major themes in German history which he felt had been obscured by the ideological and methodological shortcomings of traditional historiography: first, the origins and nature of the bureaucratic state in Prussia, and second, the evolution of foreign and military policy during the imperial era. The essays in *Der Primat der Innenpolitik* which are concerned with these themes will be the subject of this review.

In his studies of the evolution of the Beamtenstaat, Kehr confronted problems whose importance has been underscored by the work of some of Germany's finest historians and sociologists. Perhaps Kehr's approach to the history of the bureaucracy in Germany can best be defined by contrasting it with that of Otto Hintze, who studied the development of the Prussian administration with such skill and admiration in the years before 1914. Hintze's work was informed by his devotion to the Prussian state; he saw the bureaucracy as both the source and the substance of Prussia's greatness. In his mind, the distinctive feature of the German political system was the transcendence of the bureaucratic state over society, which enabled political authority to remain above the conflict of

---

[1] Kehr's most sustained discussion of the German historiographical tradition is his previously unpublished essay "Modern German Historiography," pp. 254–68.

socio-economic interests.[2] Kehr, on the other hand, sought to understand not Prussia's historical rise to power, but the unwholesome hegemony of the bureaucracy in republican Germany. He viewed the development of the administration not as part of Prussia's triumph, but as part of the German Bürgertum's defeat. His point of departure was not the transcendence of the state over society, but rather the deep involvement of the bureaucracy in the defense of certain socio-economic interests against the forces of social and political democratization.[3]

Like many other students of the problem, Kehr turned to the era of Prussian reforms for the key events in the emergence of bureaucratic power. In his essay "The Genesis of the Prussian Bureaucracy and the Rechtsstaat," he sought to study not only the origins of what Karl Mannheim called the tendency "to turn all problems of politics into problems of administration," but also the social origins and implications of the Beamtenstaat. Under Kehr's scrutiny, the reform era appeared neither as a time of idealism and national regeneration, nor as a preparation for Prussian hegemony in Germany, but rather as a period in which social and political groups became involved in a vigorous struggle for power. Kehr rejected the historical myth which regarded Freiherr vom Stein as "a liberal democrat" (p. 36). For Kehr, Stein was a "typical bureaucrat of the fading old regime," who paved the way for the primacy of bureaucratic power despite his own intellectual

---

[2] Hintze's views on the relationship of the state and society can be found in his essay on "Das monarchische Prinzip und die konstitutionelle Verfassung," reprinted in *Staat und Verfassung: Gesammelte Abhandlungen* (2nd ed. Göttingen, 1962). Needless to say, my comparison of Hintze and Kehr is not intended to denigrate the former's extraordinary contribution to our understanding of Prussian institutions.

[3] Kehr stressed the contemporary relevance of his work in his essay on "The Dictatorship of the Bureaucracy," pp. 244–53.

antipathy towards officialdom. The achievements of Stein and the other reformers were either ephemeral or disingenuous: the abolition of serfdom was a "cold and cynical sacrificing of the peasantry" (p. 246), and the much-praised Selbstverwaltung was a maneuver in the officials' scramble for power (pp. 36–37). The ideologies of conservative romanticism and the liberal Rechtsstaat were smokescreens designed to conceal the pursuit of special interests (pp. 40–41). Kehr devoted particular attention to the notion of the Rechtsstaat, which he regarded as at once a weapon of the bureaucracy against the residual powers of the nobility and as a means for the Bürgertum's economic self-aggrandizement. Unfortunately, we do not know how Kehr extended this analysis in his work on the reformers' financial policies, although it is clear that he intended to emphasize the role of bankers and other economic interest groups during the reform era.[4]

Kehr's analysis of the reformers is an intellectually powerful antidote for the two-dimensional portraits too often found in patriotic historiography. At times, however, the provocative tone of Kehr's argument, which gave such energy and verve to his work, led him to obvious exaggeration. Surely Kehr goes too far, for example, when he remarks that all of the Bürgertum's political aspirations were motivated by economic ambition (p. 42). Similarly, Kehr' s willingness to generalize about social groups seems to me to result in a somewhat oversimplified view of the socio-economic conflicts in the early nineteenth century. Perhaps the strengths and weaknesses of Kehr' s account can be suggested by mentioning two recent authors who also discuss the origins of the Beamtenstaat. Both Hans Rosenberg and Reinhart Koselleck share Kehr's impatience with shallow and overly idealistic views of the reformers; both emphasize the importance of the struggles for

---

[4] For hints of Kehr's hypothesis, see the quotations from his letters given in Wehler's introduction (pp. 11ff) and the fragment "Money and War in the Age of Mechanical Revolution," pp. 206–9.

power and profit on which Kehr focused. However, Rosenberg and Koselleck have a rather sharper eye for nuances in social change, for the subtleties in the interplay of ideologies and interests, of the state and society.[5]

Three years before the appearance of his essay on the reform era, Kehr published "The Social System of Reaction under the Puttkamer Ministry," in which he examined the relationship between the bureaucracy and the social structure during the imperial period. In the 1870's, Kehr argued, the three-way struggle among the Bürgertum, aristocracy, and bureaucracy, which had marked the first two thirds of the nineteenth century, was replaced by a new conflict between the proletariat and the propertied classes. This new structure of social conflict led to an axial shift in German domestic politics at the end of the seventies: the passage of the anti-Socialist law and social welfare legislation, the introduction of protective tariffs, and a shift in recruitment policies within the state apparatus. It was with this last development that the career of Robert von Puttkamer is linked. Kehr traced how, under Puttkamer's leadership, the Prussian bureaucracy placed increasing emphasis on political reliability within its ranks, which entailed an endorsement of "neo-feudal" values as well as an unequivocal acceptance of the empire's social and political structure. The bureaucracy thereby became a means of institutionalizing the realignment of social forces which gathered to defend the established order against the danger of Socialism. In a particularly brilliant analysis, Kehr showed how this socio-political realignment was accompanied by an ideological mobilization in defense of the status quo: in the primary schools, this took the form of a renewed emphasis on the conservative lessons of religious orthodoxy; for the

---

[5] Hans Rosenberg, *Bureaucracy, Aristocracy, and Autocracy: The Prussian Experience, 1660–1815* (Cambridge, Mass., 1958) and Reinhart Koselleck, *Preussen zwischen Reform und Revolution* (Stuttgart, 1967).

Gebildeten, there were the more sophisticated and up-to-date arguments of jurists like Laband and historians like Treitschke.

Kehr's essay on Puttkamer seems to me to be more flexible and subtle than his later work on the reform era. In fact, his later tendency to question the authenticity of progressive impulses in the bureaucracy somewhat weakens the force of his analysis of Puttkamer's significance. Thus it is difficult to take seriously Kehr's remark that Puttkamer was only slightly less important than Bismarck for German history (p. 65) if we accept his later statement that the liberal judiciary "almost automatically" embraced neo-feudal attitudes during the imperial period (p. 50).

In any event, Kehr's emphasis on the significance of the changes effected in German politics and society at the end of the 1870's has found increasing resonance in recent scholarship. Rudolf Morsey, for example, has pointed to a parallel growth in the pressure for political conformity among the imperial bureaucracy, while Hans Rosenberg and Helmut Böhme have helped to illuminate the socio-economic setting for the process of Entliberalisierung which Kehr described.[6]

Kehr's well-known essay on "The Origins of the Prussian Reserve Officer Corps" treated many of the same themes as his Puttkamer article. Kehr argued that the formation of the reserve officer corps was the historical analogue of the bureaucracy's personnel policies at the end of the 1870's: both were produced by a regrouping of social forces against the proletariat, both were designed to strengthen the commitment of the Bürgertum to the status quo by encouraging the assimilation of neofeudal values. An essay entitled "Class Conflict and Armaments Policy in Imperial Germany" extended this discussion of the army's recruitment patterns by

---

[6] Rudolf Morsey, *Die Oberste Reichsverwaltung unter Bismarck, 1867–1890* (Münster, 1957), pp. 262ff; Hans Rosenberg, *Grosse Depression und Bismarckzeit* (Berlin, 1967); and Helmut Böhme, *Deutschlands Weg zur Grossmacht* (Cologne and Berlin, 1966).

showing that resistance to an expansion of the army on the eve
of the First World War came not from military considerations
but from anxieties about the domestic implications of an
enlarged and therefore more socially diversified officer corps.
In this same article, Kehr tried to demonstrate that even
strategy was dictated by domestic considerations. He did this
with some success in his discussion of the navy, whose leaders
often presented naval expansion as a "Funktion der
Seeinteressen." Rather less convincing was his effort to show
that the General Staff's commitment to a brief, decisive war
was a reflection of the capitalist social setting. However, by
raising the general problem of the relationship between
military policy and economic developments, Kehr suggested a
number of potentially fruitful lines of historical inquiry, some
of which have been followed with great success by Gerald
Feldman in his book *Army, Industry, and Labor in Germany,
1914–1918* (Princeton, 1966).

Kehr's argument that military policy was not the result of a
rational assessment of the national interest was one prong of
his frontal assault on the notion of the "primacy of foreign
policy." Like strategy, diplomacy was not a response to the
moves of a foreign power, not a high-stakes chess game
between opposing statesmen, but rather was the reflection of
internal social conflict. Kehr maintained that to overlook the
social roots of foreign affairs and to become lost in the day-to-
day exchange of dispatches was to indulge in a myopic
scholarship which reinforced the reactionary political ideology
of the Machtstaat.

In a series of extremely stimulating articles, Kehr examined
German foreign policy in the 1890's in order to elucidate the
social basis of diplomacy. In "The Social and Financial Basis
of Tirpitz's Propaganda," Kehr provided one of the first
detailed accounts of the effect of interest groups on the making
of foreign policy, an issue still largely neglected by historians.
Kehr's evidence suggests that the major support for the
Flottenverein was motivated by a search for profits, not by the

patriotic phrases so often used to justify the fleet. Of particular
value is Kehr's analysis of Tirpitz' s role in tying the expansion
of the navy to key issues on the German domestic scene. "The
German Fleet in the 1890's and the Political-Military Dualism
of the Empire" demonstrates how Tirpitz sought to break out
of the dichotomy between political and military authority by
engaging the Reichstag in the support of the fleet through an
appeal to the interests and anxieties of the Bürgertum. Kehr's
analysis of the fleet, like his work on the army and the
bureaucracy, emphasized the significance of an alliance among
propertied elites against the proletariat. Thus the final passage
of the second naval bill was the result of a socio-political
arrangement by which industrial and agricultural interests
supported both naval expansion and protective tariffs as one
facet of their common defense of the established order against
the left. It was also in terms of this alliance that Kehr viewed
the failure of British and German diplomats to reach some
agreement on the issues which divided their nations.[7] He
believed opposition to England was prompted by domestic
considerations: for the Bürgertum, England was an economic
competitor and a threat to German Weltpolitik; for the landed
nobility, England was "the advanced capitalist model of
[Germany's] own industrial development" (p. 181). The logical
corollary to the failure of an alliance with Britain, Kehr felt,
was some kind of understanding with Russia. But social forces
precluded the operation of this diplomatic logic because the
landed elite's need for agricultural tariffs resulted in a
permanent alienation of the Russians. Germany's diplomatic
isolation, therefore, did not come from the envy and animosity
of her neighbors, nor even from the incompetence of her
statesmen, but was a foreign political necessity dictated by the
socio-political alignment upon which imperial Germany rested.

---

[7] See "Hatred of England and World Politics" and "The Problem of
an Anglo-German Alliance at the Turn of the Century."

The alliance between Bürgertum and nobility is one of the most significant themes in *Der Primat der Innenpolitik*. Recent scholarship has reaffirmed the importance of this theme, but also has revised Kehr's formulation of it. For example, in his monograph on *Industrielle Interessenpolitik in der wilhelminischen Gesellschaft* (Berlin, 1967), Hartmut Kaelble traces the development of an increasing diversity of ideology and interest within the industrial establishment, which requires a certain refinement of some of Kehr's social categories. Moreover, Kaelble demonstrates that a number of industrialists were overtly hostile to cooperation with landed interests and that by 1914 this opposition makes it difficult to speak of an effective alliance between "Junkerdom and heavy industry."[8] Similarly, Hans-Jürgen Puhle's important work on *Agrarische Interessenpolitik und preussischer Konservatismus im wilhelminischen Reich* (Hanover, 1966) suggests centrifugal forces in the relationship between the Bürgertum and the landed elites. Although Puhle acknowledges his debt to Kehr, he points out that Kehr greatly overestimated the continuity and stability of the industrial-agrarian bloc. Just as there were industrialists who opposed cooperation with the agrarians, so there were elements in the Bund der Landwirte which would not make the compromises necessary for a working arrangement with industrial interests.[9]

More important than the refinements which might be added to Kehr's image of the relationship between the Bürgertum and agrarian elites are the methodological problems suggested by some of the essays in this volume. In the first place, Kehr never made clear where he stood on the relative importance of domestic affairs for the direction of foreign policy. At times, he seemed to say only that foreign and domestic politics are inseparable. Elsewhere, he went further and suggested that domestic concerns are usually more important than diplomatic

---

[8] Kaelble, p. 146.
[9] See Puhle, pp. 155–64, especially p. 158, n. 94.

considerations. And occasionally he asserted a rather doctrinaire "primacy of domestic policy," which seems to me difficult to justify except through some historical metaphysics in which Kehr did not believe. In part, this inconsistency arises from the consciously provocative character of Kehr's style. But it is more than stylistic excess and must be seen as the result of a methodological imprecision which is the most important weakness in Kehr's work. A second manifestation of this imprecision can be found in Kehr's view of the individual's role in historical change. As I have mentioned, some of the finest sections in these essays deal with the significance of men like Puttkamer and Tirpitz for German history. However, at one point in his essay on "Class Conflict and Armament Policy in Imperial Germany," he remarked: "The participants believe they are acting, but they are doing nothing through their intrigues but bringing about what was ordained by the alignment of social forces" (p. 110, see also p. 180). Did Kehr actually believe in the kind of social determinism implied by this statement? Did he regard individuals as the pawns of impersonal social forces? There is a great deal in his work to suggest that he did not. But the inconsistency remains and calls attention to his failure to clarify his position on the relationship between individuals and social forces. A final methodological imprecision concerns the role of socio-economic interests. Here again Kehr was inconsistent. In some passages he showed great skill in portraying the interaction of social, economic, and ideological factors. At times, however, he seemed willing to reduce behavior to a monocausal economic explanation (e.g., p.151). One can regret these flaws in the logic of Kehr's inquiry, but at the same time recognize that such exaggerations were perhaps the unavoidable byproduct of Kehr' s reaction against the German historiographical tradition which overemphasized the importance of foreign policy, the individual, and ideology in effecting historical change. Moreover, it should be noted that if his style lent itself to exaggeration, it also reflected an imaginative intensity and an intellectual daring which gave Kehr's scholarship extraordinary freshness and vigor.

Whatever revisions must be made in the substance of Kehr's work and whatever questions must be raised about inconsistencies in his method, there is no doubt that he formulated basic problems and employed modes of analysis which illuminate the past and suggest avenues for future research. Equally important, Kehr is a model for the historian who refuses to cater to his nation's urge for self-idealization, but instead sees his function as that of a social critic committed to uncovering the disparity between pretension and reality. It is encouraging to note that an increasing number of scholars in Germany are considering the same problems Kehr defined, not only in the light of his methodological insights but also from the same critical perspective. The work of these men is an appropriate monument to the energy and skill which characterized Eckart Kehr' s commitment to both scholarship and social progress.

8

Mack Walker's *German Home Towns*[*]

In order to understand fully Mack Walker's achievement in *German Home Towns*, it is necessary to recall the historiographical context within which it was written. By the late 1960s, what would come to be called the Sonderweg interpretation of German history was firmly in place. This interpretation had four characteristics. First, its geographical focus was on Prussia, the state that patriotic scholars in the nineteenth century had praised as the demiurge of national unification but that critical historians after 1945 blamed for the catastrophes of war and dictatorship. Second, its substantive focus was on state institutions, once regarded as the source of Germany's national power and progress, now viewed as instruments of foreign aggression and internal repression. Third, its methodological focus tended to be on politics and ideology, although, again in contrast to nineteenth-century historiography, these were seen not as autonomous elements, but as products of social and economic forces. Finally and most important, the Sonderweg interpretation took as its point

[*]Published as the introduction to the Cornell University Press paperback edition of *German Home Towns: Community, State, and General Estate* (Ithaca, 1998), pp. xii–xvii. The book was first published by Cornell in 1971.

of departure Germany's apparent deviation from the West, a deviation that explained, so these historians argued, both the failure of German democracy and the success of National Socialism. Among the alleged differences between German history and the western model, none was more consequential than the absence of a strong bourgeoisie that could have successfully wrested control of state and society away from representatives of the old regime. Because the German bourgeoisie did not fulfill this historical mission, tectonic strains developed within Germany's social and political system, strains that eventually produced the accelerating series of crises that culminated in Hitler's Third Reich.

Although Walker's book also ends with the rise of Nazism, his path to 1933 takes us through a very different historical landscape. Geographically, Prussia is on the periphery rather than at the center of his story; it is present as a foil to the "individualized country" where his home towns could flourish beyond the reaches of any single state's power. Like Prussia, the state itself is on the margins of Walker's main story; instead of praising or indicting the uses of state power, he traces a different kind of politics, smaller in scale, less formally articulated, usually indistinguishable from other aspects of community life. When bureaucrats appear in *German Home Towns*, they come as neither heroes nor villains, but as outsiders, who are temperamentally incapable of understanding a world in which their rules and procedures do not apply. Although Walker considers both the theory and practice of bureaucratic politics, he does so in terms of its impact on the towns. Methodologically, this required that he look beyond the source materials upon which most German history had been based. Instead of concentrating on philosophical treatises (that tell us what the state should do) or bureaucratic regulations (that tell us what the state wanted to do), Walker turned to an archival study of local communities where he could find evidence about what the state was actually able to accomplish. In contrast to the prevailing historiographical fashion, therefore, Walker did not write about the intellectual or institutional nature of politics, but rather about the impact of political action on community life and social experience.

Walker's moves away from German historiography's geographical, substantive, and methodological conventions were in the service of his central purpose, which was, as he puts it in his characteristically modest and unobtrusive introduction, to write a book "not about the liberal bourgeoisie that Germany did not get, but about the hometown Bürgerschaft that Germany preeminently did get." A full decade before the critical assault on the Sonderweg interpretation began, Walker grasped its major flaw. Those who explain Germany's problems by showing what is not there, he gently suggests, "suffer from coming at the problem backwards, so that they stand history on its head. They assume a proper historical pattern and then punish the phenomena for their unwillingness to conform." In order to set German historiography back on its feet, Walker must show that "the German hometown Burger was not a pale, underdeveloped imitation of the bourgeois who figures so prominently in modem European history; he was something quite different and even antithetical in principle, a distinction badly garbled by the term 'petty bourgeois.'"

German Home Towns is a social biography of the hometown Bürger, from the end of the seventeenth to the beginning of the twentieth centuries. After his opening chapters on the political, social, and economic basis of town life, Walker traces a painful process of decline that, while occasionally slowed or diverted, leads inexorably toward death and, in the twentieth century, transfiguration. Along the way we learn a great many new things about local government, corporate economies, and communal society. Equally important, we see a great many familiar issues in new and compelling ways. Walker's picture of the Holy Roman Empire, for example, differed dramatically from the ramshackle, faintly ridiculous anachronism that appeared in most historical accounts. Similarly, the Napoleonic reforms and the revolution of 1848, which had usually been subsumed into the history of German nation building, take on a quite different historical meaning when viewed from the home towns' perspective. Finally, Walker suggests a new appreciation of German liberalism's underlying problem, which was to define a meaning of freedom that would make sense to both the "movers and doers" at the center and the citizens of the home towns. In the book's difficult and sometimes elusive final chapter, Walker traces the historical extinction of the towns and their transformation into ideology. From the memory of the towns, he argues, comes Germans' "ubiquitous yearning for organic wholeness," which was to have its most sinister expression in National Socialism's false promise of a racial community.

Several of the themes in *German Home Towns* have been developed in recent work on German history. Walker's revisionist view of the Holy Roman Empire, for example, is now widely accepted. His interest in local developments and in the areas outside of Prussia has sparked a number of important works. At the same time, it is clear that some recent scholarly trends would have led Walker to write a different sort of book if he had begun *German Home Towns* today. For one thing, he would have had to say more about the role of gender in community life; for another, he would probably want to pay more attention to the outsiders, the vagrants, petty criminals, and charity cases who did not participate in town life and tend to drop out of sight in his account. It is also likely that recent research on demographic patterns would help him define more precisely the scale and distribution of home towns.

But while this book—like any other—would have to be revised and perhaps reshaped by almost thirty years of new scholarship, *German Home Towns* retains a remarkable freshness and vibrancy. It is filled with interesting ideas and striking insights—on cameralism, the baroque, Biedermeier culture, legal history, and much more. In addition to the inner workings of community life, we learn about political theorists like Justi and Hegel, historians like Savigny and Eichhorn, philologists like Grimm. Well before it was fashionable, Walker was sensitive to the nuance of language, the changing status of written texts, and the diversity of discourses. He is alert to powerful long-term trends—the rise of bureaucratic states, the impact of population growth, the expansion of markets—and no less sensitive to the textures of everyday life. His few pages on the romantic aspirations of the tinsmith Flegel, citizen of Hildesheim, are a model of social analysis because of his skillful fusion of individual experience and long-range developments. The chapter on Weissenburg is a tour de force, which covers with extraordinary grace and economy material that is rich enough to support an independent monograph.

Much of the book's distinctive charm comes from Walker's straightforward and unpretentious style, a style that always seeks to clarify rather than complicate its subject, to engage rather than impress its reader. Walker is able to bring us along with him as he works his way through the material, to help us share both the challenge and pleasures of his enterprise. Consider, for example, the footnote on page 252, in which he quotes the marginal comment in Cornell Library's copy of Eichhorn's history of German law and thus provides a perfect emblem for the passage of the home towns into Germans' cultural consciousness.

Like all truly great history, *German Home Towns* is a deeply personal book, inspired by the author's profound sympathy with the human dimensions of his subject. Although there are moments when Walker seems to idealize the towns, he knows that they could be repressive and suffocating. But for all their imperfections, Walker displays both empathy and affection for the world of the home towns because in it people had a settled identity, a place, a home—because the home town was, to repeat Walker's telling quotation from Robert Frost, "the place where, when you go there, they have to take you in." The home towns are part of a lost world, but because they incorporated deep human needs, the shadow of their memory lingers, the cost of their passing is still being counted.[1]

---

[1] For an astute analysis of Walker's historiographical legacy, see Christopher R. Friedrichs, "But Are We Any Closer to Home? Early Modern German Urban History since *German Home Towns*," *Central European History*, 30, no. 2 (1997): pp. 163–86.

9

Carl Schorske at Berkeley[*]

Among the few lecture notes that have survived from my many years of formal education are six tattered pages with the dates Wednesday, October 7, and Friday, October 9, 1959. The course was Raymond J. Sontag's "Intellectual History of Europe," the place, Room 155, Dwinelle Hall, the subject, Hegel, and the lecturer, Carl E. Schorske—who had been invited to fill in while Ray Sontag was out of town. Together with the other graduate student assistants in the course, I had awaited Schorske's appearance with interest and anticipation. Of course, we did not know that this would mark the beginning of his association with Berkeley and, for some of us, of four decades of friendship, but we had heard a good deal about him. He was supposed to be a brilliant teacher, his book on Social Democracy was required reading for every serious student of German history, and we had heard rumors that he had turned down offers from both Berkeley and Harvard in order to stay at Wesleyan, decisions that seemed, to me at least, somewhat noble and very eccentric.

---

[*]Written in November 1999 as an introduction to Carl Schorske's oral history interviews. The interviews are available online: U.C. Library Digital Collections, Oral History Project, UCB History Department.

Even without the aid of my notes, I have a vivid recollection of Carl's two lectures on Hegel, which displayed his characteristic blend of rhetorical power and intellectual energy. Without losing sight of the text at hand (Hegel's lectures on the philosophy of history), he established connections between Hegel and his historical setting, explained the cultural traditions within which he worked, and then suggested the implications of his ideas for the evolution of German thought. But what made these two lectures and the many others I heard after Carl began teaching at Berkeley so memorable was not simply Carl's command of the material and his verbal brilliance, but also his ability to invite his listeners to join him and thus to transform them from his audience into his companions on a shared intellectual journey. There was always a certain openness and spontaneity in Schorske's lectures; rather than present a finished product they illustrated an ongoing inquiry. This was, I think, the most important source of the excitement with which his lecture room was always charged.

As a graduate teacher, Carl had the same ability to inform, engage, and inspire, and always to do so without arrogance or intimidation. I remember our first conversation about my ideas (if that is what my random inclinations and inchoate ambitions can be called) for a dissertation. Rather than suggesting possible topics or simply assigning me something to work on, Carl told me about the books he had recently read that seemed to suggest new and interesting ways of thinking about intellectual history: Kaegi's biography of Burckhardt, Gollwitzer's book on the Standesherren, and a few others. Clearly I was not going to be able to write such books (in fact, at that point I was barely able to read them), but he offered them to me as sources of stimulation and inspiration, models towards which to strive. This made me feel like a colleague, with whom he could share his current enthusiasms, and not like a pupil in need of direction. As my own research plans began to form, then collapsed, and finally jelled, he was always attentive, sometimes critical but never intrusive, overbearing, or discouraging. He was, moreover, extremely diligent in the quotidian dimensions of the graduate teacher's responsibilities—writing letters of recommendation, returning draft chapters, and the like—the difficulties of which I now understand and appreciate much better than I did at the time.

When Carl came to Berkeley, his scholarly reputation rested on his book about German Social Democracy, which sought to explain the party's split in 1917 in terms of deeply rooted structural and ideological divisions within the labor movement. Although I am now somewhat skeptical about the book's central argument (it seems to me that the immediate impact of the war played a more important role in the party's divisions than Carl's structural analysis would suggest), it is still one of the books I most like to read with my graduate students. It is, in the first place, a beautifully conceived and powerfully sustained historical analysis, clearly written, elegantly researched, and filled with well-chosen examples. Moreover— and this is always the sign of first-rate history—it tells us about much more than its ostensible subject: in this case, about the political and social problems of the German Empire, the interaction of ideology and organization, and last but not least, the political climate in which the book itself was written. Although after this book, Carl moved away from political history, politics always remained central to his scholarly vocation, which was indelibly marked by the two central crises of his generation: the rise of National Socialism in the thirties, which shadowed his years as an undergraduate as well as his wartime service with the OSS, and the emergence of the Cold War in the forties and early fifties, which shaped his own relationship to American politics.

By the time Carl arrived in Berkeley, he had already begun to work on culture in Vienna around the turn of the century. I recall hearing him describe this project to a packed audience of faculty and students in the Alumni House; parts of it appeared in his course on European Intellectual History, which I audited in 1960–61. For a variety of reasons—not least among them Carl's engagement with the events that are described in what follows—the book he planned to write was never written in the narrative form he had originally intended. Instead, he produced a series of essays that were eventually published in 1980 as *Fin-de-Siècle Vienna*, a book that has been widely and deeply influential across the usual disciplinary boundaries. The connecting themes uniting these essays are the collapse of Austrian liberalism and the rise of cultural modernism, which worked together to generate an unresolved tension between political pathology and cultural creativity. In *Fin-de-Siècle Vienna*, and in the many essays that he has written since (some now collected as *Thinking with History* [Princeton University Press, 1998]), Carl Schorske has illuminated the complex connections between politics and culture, his major concern as a scholar and, for the years that he was at Berkeley, the object of his efforts as an academic citizen caught up in the affairs of a great university in crisis.

10

Saul Friedländer

Saul Friedländer was born in Prague in late 1932, just four months before Hitler became the chancellor of Germany. His childhood was shadowed by the darkening cloud of anti-Semitism, especially in Hitler's Germany but extending from there across the continent. In March 1939, on the eve of the German invasion of Prague, Friedländer and family fled to France. Here, following his parents' deportation and murder, he spent the war in hiding. Pavel became Paul, a devout young Catholic, whose survival depended on concealing, perhaps even from himself, who and what he was. In the spring of 1948, he left France and arrived in Palestine just as the state of Israel was founded. Pavel, once Paul, now became Saul.

Friedländer tells the story of his childhood in *When Memory Comes* (New York, 1979), which is one of the most remarkable autobiographies of the century. Weaving together different strands of time—Prague in the thirties, France in the forties, Israel in the seventies—Friedländer explores the complexity of identity, the bonds of family and tradition, and, above all, the overwhelming sense of loss that must attend our efforts to

Previously unpublished. Written as an introduction to Saul Friedländer's lecture at Stanford on 27 November 2007.

understand the Holocaust. Here is his description of leaving Prague with his parents: "The more time passes, the more I feel that it is there, in this earliest setting of my life, rather than in the terrible upheavals that followed, that the essential part of my self was shaped."

Friedländer took the title of his autobiography—and its epigraph—from a novel by the Prague writer Gustav Meyrink: "When knowledge comes, memory comes too, little by little. Knowledge and memory are one and same thing." In his autobiography, of course, knowledge and memory serve the same end, a search for self as it is revealed along life's trajectory. But in an important sense, the complex relationship between knowledge and memory has shaped all of Friedländer's work and, most especially, his masterpiece, *Nazi Germany and the Jews*. The first volume, covering the years of persecution from 1933 to 1939, was published in 1997, the second, on the years of extermination, appeared earlier this year.

These two volumes, the product of almost twenty years of reading and research, rest on an extraordinary knowledge of the scholarly literature and primary sources—but this knowledge is lightly worn, always sufficiently displayed but never intrusive. Experts will recognize how much effort went into Friedländer's summary of a particular issue, but every reader will—as the author intends—be carried away by the human dimensions of his story. And these dimensions depend less on knowledge than on memory.

The book's structure is deceptively simple: Across a strict chronological organization, Friedländer has stretched the first-hand accounts of perpetrators and, especially, of victims, whose recorded experiences—usually interrupted by death—give the account its emotional power and personality. His achievement is to let these voices speak, selecting and arranging them in ways that move the story, extend its range, suggest its depth and variety. The result is a monument to both knowledge and memory, a scholarly masterpiece that helps us to confront what will always be the great challenge in understanding the Holocaust, which is to grasp both its immensity and specificity.

11

Gordon A. Craig[*]

In the spring of 1936, Gordon A. Craig, twenty-two years old and about to graduate from Princeton, made two of his earliest public appearances. The first was a poem, modeled on a Latin Ode, published in the *Nassau Lit* with the title "Marxicos Odi," and dedicated "To My Proletarian Sweetheart." The poem evokes the brevity of life, the swift passing of undergraduate pleasures, and their irresistible distraction from more serious things:

> Granted we are a feckless crew;
> But can you lift your voice to scold
> If social questions leave us cold
> When spring comes barging in anew?

A few weeks later, a somewhat different Gordon Craig delivered the Valedictory Address to the class of 1936. A sense of political crisis loomed large in these remarks, of problems too long neglected and perils soon to come. The young valedictorian saw much more clearly than most Americans that "in the next few years, as a world power, [America] may have to make grave decisions as to her attitude toward belligerent nations in other parts of the world." Evoking a speech by

[*]Published in *Central European History*, 40, no. 1 (March 2007): pp. 133–37.

Woodrow Wilson delivered forty years before, Craig urged his classmates to devote themselves to the nation's pressing business, not in order to further change for the sake of change, but to foster growth and progress, "for intellectual growth is conservative of life, and progress is life itself."

In his valedictory remarks Craig pointed to events in Germany as an example of what liberalism's failure can produce. The preceding summer he had observed the German situation firsthand when he spent two months studying and traveling there with a group of Princeton undergraduates. His journal from this trip provides a remarkably clear-headed and insightful picture of the Nazi regime, then two years in power, its hold on political institutions and on popular loyalties virtually unchallenged, but its future development still obscure. Especially striking are his reports of a series of conversations about the "Jewish question"—often with people who claimed to wish the Jews no harm but were trying to understate or explain away the rising tide of persecution against them. Here we see examples of that toxic blend of delusion and deceit which would help to pave the road to catastrophe that lay ahead.

These experiences in the summer of 1935 began—and in some ways permanently marked—Craig's extraordinarily productive personal and intellectual engagement with Germans and Germany. But his time in Germany had a more direct and immediate result for Craig's future: a chance meeting with a Rhodes scholar, who sang the praises of Oxford, led him to apply for a scholarship, which, much to his surprise, he won. He arrived at Balliol College in the fall of 1936 to spend two of the most important years of his life. In Oxford, Craig studied with B. H. Sumner and E. L. Woodward, two of Britain's finest historians, deepened his knowledge and experience of Europe, and watched from a ringside seat the preliminary bouts for the major European war that everyone expected.

"Craig is a small white-haired American," wrote Dan Davin about the young scholar from New Jersey, "with a good brain, sensibility, a rich deep voice and deeper humour." Together with Davin, Walt Rostow, Philip Kaiser, and many others, Craig became a well-known figure on the Oxford scene, much sought after in Junior Common Rooms for his songs and no stranger to Oxford's many pubs. It was also during his time at Oxford that Craig met Phyllis Halcomb, a young American staying with her English aunt. They would soon become engaged, marry, and be together for the next sixty-six years. Despite a strenuous social life—many long night conversations on literature and life with his friends, lots of music, and various excursions to London and Paris, all washed down with not inconsiderable quantities of drink—Craig worked extremely hard at Oxford, producing a thesis for his B.Litt. on British policy in the Luxemburg crisis of 1867. Some of his drinking companions found this subject rather hilarious, but the thesis is, in fact, a fine piece of work, still a journeyman's work, but one in which the master's talents as an historian and as a stylist are already apparent.

After two years in Oxford, Craig returned to Princeton, where he worked with Raymond James Sontag, a legendary teacher and scholar, who had just published a masterful study of *Germany and England*, in which he sought to define the cultural basis of their fateful antagonism. Although he had been trained as a medievalist, Sontag made his reputation as a diplomatic historian—his survey of European diplomacy, first published in 1933, is still very much worth reading. He was also a fine stylist with broad literary and cultural interests—it was Sontag, for instance, who recommended the book that began Craig's long fascination with Theodor Fontane.

Craig's dissertation, written under Sontag's direction and finished in the spring of 1941, was entitled "Britain and Europe, 1866–69: A Study in the Application of Non-Intervention." It included a chapter on the Luxemburg crisis, but set the events from his Oxford thesis in the broader context of the British response to the diplomatic revolution that began with Prussia's victory over Austria in 1866 and ended with the defeat of France in 1870. Although Craig wrote this analysis of Britain's ambivalent relationship to European affairs during the most critical stage of the Second World War, he carefully avoided any cheaply bought connections to current events. This scholarly restraint made the connection between his story and its contemporary setting all the more compelling.

After teaching at Yale for a year, Craig returned to Princeton in 1941 to take the position left vacant by Sontag's departure for the University of California at Berkeley. A few months later Craig was drawn into the war, first with the OSS, then the Marine corps. Returning to Princeton from service in the Pacific, his rise through the academic ranks was rapid: in response to an offer from Cornell in the spring of 1946, he was promoted to Associate Professor; other offers and promotion to full professor followed. In 1961, Craig—much to the surprise of his colleagues—moved from Princeton to Stanford. From 1969 until this retirement in 1985, he was the J. E. Wallace Sterling Professor in the Humanities.

At both Princeton and Stanford, Craig was extraordinarily successful in the classroom. Beautifully written and flawlessly delivered, his lectures introduced generations of students to the drama of European history. He had a distinguished group of doctoral students, many of whom went on to be leaders of the profession: at the time of his death, the president and executive secretary of the German Studies Association, and the editor of the *German Studies Review* all received their PhD's under his direction.

It is not surprising that Craig began as a diplomatic historian and continued to invest much of his time and energy in the study of international relations. Not only his own teacher, but the most talented members of Sontag's generation had devoted themselves to examining the diplomatic origins of the First World War and thus of America's own entrance into European affairs: Sidney Fay (whose revisionist work on the origins of the war was one of the first important American contributions to modern European history), William Langer, Bernadotte Schmitt, and many others made diplomacy, seen in a European context, their major concern. During the first ten years of its existence, from 1929 to 1939, *The Journal of Modern History* published 37 articles on modern Europe, of which 23 were about some aspect of diplomacy.

Like his teachers, Craig tried to understand the structure of nineteenth-century politics—best illustrated perhaps by his brilliant contribution to the *New Cambridge Modern History*. But he also brought to the subject a new set of concerns. He became, for instance, a master of the biographical approach to diplomacy, which he used as the coeditor of, and contributor to, *The Diplomats*, a classic collection of biographies of statesmen and ambassadors between the wars, and in his marvelous synthesis of German foreign policy from Bismarck to Adenauer, which began as a series of lectures at Johns Hopkins. Craig also developed an interest in the military dimensions of international relations, which led him to his first major work, *The Politics of the Prussian Army*, which he published in 1955. In this book, Craig moved confidently across two hundred years of German history, tracing the evolution of the Prussian army from its origins as an instrument of seventeenth-century absolutism to its final degradation and defeat in the Second World War.

Craig's intellectual temperament was shaped by Anglo-American liberalism, perhaps most of all by the great figures of the Scottish enlightenment. His literary style was nourished by his deep reading of British literature: William Hazlitt, whom he especially admired, but also Dickens, P. G. Wodehouse, and many others. Very early in his career, Craig developed a characteristic mode of expression, apparent in both his writing and his public presentations: clear, graceful, beautifully balanced sentences, a wide range of literary allusions, an eye for the right quotation and telling detail—all aimed at communicating with both his fellow scholars and the lay audience, "from which" he once said, "we ultimately derive our legitimacy."

Craig had many interests and wrote on many subjects, but he returned again and again to the German question, that is, the question of how a culture and society so rich in promise and accomplishment could have produced one of history's most murderously destructive regimes. In the last, extraordinarily productive decades of his life, he wrestled with different aspects of this question: in *The History of Germany, 1866–1945*, his magisterial contribution to the Oxford History of Modern Europe Series, in his brilliantly evocative book on *The Germans*, and in scores of articles and essays, especially for the *New York Review of Books*. His last book, a study of the great German novelist Theodor Fontane, was a labor of love: beautifully written and elegant constructed, it was infused with the author's deep sympathy for his subject. All of the work from this stage of his career was translated and published by Beck Verlag, whose editors became his close friends and admirers. These translations were not only a great critical and commercial success, they made him something of a celebrity in Germany, where he was the subject of television programs and magazine articles.

From his selection as valedictorian in 1936 until his death, Craig's accomplishments were recognized by numerous awards and prizes. He was a member of the Academy of Arts and Sciences and the American Philosophical Society, a fellow of the British Academy, an Honorary Fellow of Balliol College, and a member of the Orden Pour le Mèrite für Wissenschaften und Künste. He served as president of the American Historical Association and vice-president of the Comité International des Sciences Historiques. He was awarded the Commander's Cross of the Legion of Merit by the Federal Republic of Germany, Goethe Medaille by the Goethe Gesellschaft, and the Benjamin Franklin-Wilhelm von Humboldt Prize by the German-American Academic Council.

For more than sixty years, Craig kept a diary, which is now available in the Stanford Library; plans to publish portions of it are currently underway. Although the diary is not complete—some of the years are summarized in the form of a memoir based on pocket diaries and recollections—it nonetheless provides a vivid portrait of Craig's active, energetic career. Family and friends play a big role, but there is also a lot about teaching, new books read and old ones rediscovered, research projects, lectures, university affairs, and government service. Reading this diary and reflecting on his long and productive life, one is reminded of what Wilhelm Dilthey, the great German philosopher and historian of ideas, once described as "the foundation of historical vision." This vision comes, Dilthey wrote, "from the power and breadth of our own lives and the energy with which we reflect upon them. It is this vision alone that enables us to give life back to the bloodless shadows of the past."

Gordon Craig remained intellectually active until the final months of his life, when first his eyesight, then his heart failed. But even after his world had shrunk to a hospital room and blindness had separated him from the written words he loved so much, he somehow remained himself, capable of becoming—at least for a few minutes—that deep-voiced, deeply humorous American whom Dan Davin had first encountered in Balliol's inner quad seventy years before.

Gordon Craig died on October 30, 2005, in Portola Valley, California. He was survived by his wife of sixty-six years, Phyllis Halcomb Craig (who died in May 2006), by his daughters, the Reverend Susan Craig, Dr. Deborah Preston, and Professor Martha Craig, his son, Charles Craig, eight grandchildren, and two great-grandchildren.

12

Werner Thomas Angress[*]

Werner Angress was born in Berlin on June 27, 1920. He grew up in a comfortable middle-class family of assimilated German Jews. After the Nazis took power in 1933, his life was shadowed by the darkening cloud of anti-Semitism and the growing sense that Germany, the country with which he continued to identify, was no longer his. As a teenager, Angress sought refuge at Gross Breesen, a farming community near Berlin where young Jews learned the agricultural skills that were supposed to prepare them for emigration. Here, under the leadership of the community's charismatic leader, Curt Bondy, he formed friendships that would last throughout his long and eventful life. In 1937, the family fled Germany. Two years later, Werner left for the United States while the rest of his family remained in Amsterdam. His mother and two brothers survived the war in hiding; his father, arrested by Gestapo after the German invasion of the Netherlands, died in Auschwitz.

In America, Angress worked on a farm in Virginia. When he applied for citizenship, he changed his middle name from *Karl* to Thomas and from then on he would be known as Tom to most of his friends. Drafted into the army in 1941, he was trained as an interrogator at Camp Ritchie (he is featured in the

---

[*]Published in *Perspectives on History* (December 2010).

film, *The Ritchie Boys*, about this remarkable institution), and
parachuted (his first jump) into France with the 82nd Airborne
on D-Day. Despite his extraordinarily youthful appearance and
rather small stature, Tom was a tough and resourceful soldier
who was eventually promoted to Master Sergeant and awarded
the Bronze Star and the Purple Heart. In May 1945, he drove
a borrowed jeep to Amsterdam, where he was reunited with
mother and brothers, from whom he had heard nothing since
the beginning of the war.

Tom got his B.A. in History from Wesleyan University and
his Ph.D. from the University of California at Berkeley, where
he worked with Raymond J. Sontag. He taught at Berkeley and
then, for twenty-five years, at the State University of New York
at Stony Brook.

Angress's first book, based on his Berkeley dissertation, was
*Stillborn Revolution: The Communist Bid for Power in Germany, 1921–
1923* (Princeton Press, 1963, translated into German as *Die
Kampfzeit der KPD, 1921–1923* and published by Droste Verlag
in 1973). Deeply researched and forcefully argued, *Stillborn
Revolution* traces the German Communist Party's difficult
evolution as it tried to come to terms with the failure of its
revolutionary aspirations, the political vacuum left by the
murder of its most effective leaders, and the growing influence
of the Soviet Union. After fifty years, *Stillborn Revolution*
remains the standard work on German Communism in the
early Weimar Republic.

Although Angress continued to publish articles on Weimar
politics, his interests turned more and more to the history that
most powerfully shaped his own life, the history of Germany's
Jews and their long, complex, and ultimately tragic relationship
to German politics and society. Over the next three decades,
Angress produced a series of extraordinary articles. To
mention just three of them: "Juden im politischen Leben der
Revolutionszeit" (1971), "Prussia's Army and the Jewish
Reserve Officer Controversy before World War I" (1972),
and—my own favorite—"The German Army's 'Judenzählung'

of 1916: Genesis—Consequences—Significance" (1978). Unlike those books that could easily have been articles, many of Angress's articles were weighty and significant enough to have been books.

In 1965, Angress published a brief essay in the *Year Book of the Leo Baeck Institute* on Gross Breesen. This turned out to be the first of a number of autobiographical pieces that increasingly absorbed his energies and attention. The most significant products of this were two books. *Generation zwischen Furcht und Hoffnung: Jüdische Jugend im Dritten Reich* (Christians Verlag, 1985, translated as *Between Fear and Hope: Jewish Youth in the Third Reich* and published by Columbia University Press in 1988) begins with a long essay on the fate of young German Jews under the Nazis and then prints letters and documents about Angress's time in Gross Breesen and his heroic (and ultimately successful) efforts to save the members of the community who were arrested in 1938. Angress's last book, . . . *immer etwas abseits: Jugenderinnerungen eines jüdischen Berliners, 1920–1945* (Edition Hentrich, 2005), tells the story of his childhood, the increasingly toxic atmosphere of Nazi Berlin, his emigration, and military service. It is, in many ways, the story of sorrow and of loss, but also of resilience, courage and, ultimately, of survival, vividly illustrated by the photograph of Tom and his extended family with which the book concludes.

Throughout his long career, Tom Angress was a dedicated and effective teacher who was twice honored with prestigious awards at SUNY Stony Brook. After his retirement and return to Berlin in 1988, he continued to teach, to mentor young scholars, and to share his experiences with high school students who were growing up in a very different Berlin.

Like all of us, Tom had his faults: his temper, usually directed at the many mechanical devices that defied his will, was legendary. But to those hundreds of people whose lives he touched, Tom Angress will be remembered for his fundamental decency, tolerance, and generosity. He was an attentive and devoted friend, a thoughtful companion at times of joy and sadness. Tom's memory will be cherished by many throughout the world and especially by the family whose love was at the center of his life: his two brothers, Hans and Fred, his former wives, Millie and Claudia, his sons, Dan and Percy, his daughters, Nadine and Miriam, his daughters and sons-in-law, grandchildren, and the companion of his final years, Elma Gaasbeek.

Werner Thomas Angress died in Berlin on July 5, 2010, a week after his ninetieth birthday.

13

Hans-Ulrich Wehler[*]

Born in 1931, Hans-Ulrich Wehler was one of the most productive and influential members of a generation that played a major role in the formation of postwar Germany's political culture. This was the Hitler Youth generation, too young to be directly involved in Nazism's crimes, but old enough to know that, if the Third Reich had survived just a little longer, they would inevitably have been drawn into the regime's poisonous web. This was also the generation of exchange students. Like so many of his contemporaries, Wehler spent a formative year in the United States, in his case as an undergraduate at Ohio University in Athens, Ohio. For Wehler, as for thousands of young Germans, the experience of their time in America—this was, it is important to remember, the America of the 1950s, an America that still enjoyed the untroubled confidence of the postwar era—left an indelible mark on his political consciousness. When Wehler returned to the United States in 1963 on a fellowship, he established his long and fruitful relationship with Hans Rosenberg, a leading member of that generation of German émigré scholars who would play a vital role in the development of postwar historiography on both sides of the Atlantic. Rosenberg, who taught for many years at

[*]Published in *Perspectives on History* (October 2014).

Brooklyn College before moving to the University of California at Berkeley, remained a powerful influence on his life and work. In addition to Rosenberg, Wehler's trans-Atlantic ties were strengthened by his friendship with many other American historians, including members of the second generation of German émigrés like Klaus Epstein and Fritz Stern.

Wehler spent his formative years at the University of Cologne, where he was one of that extraordinarily gifted and diverse group of doctoral students who gathered around Theodor Schieder. As Christoph Nonn makes clear in his recent biography (*Theodor Schieder: Ein bürgerlicher Historiker im 20.Jahrhundert* [Düsseldorf, 2013]), Schieder was an inspiring and supportive mentor, willing to work with young scholars with very different political sympathies and scholarly temperaments and able to use his formidable influence to help them get positions in the rapidly-expanding German university system.

Wehler taught briefly in Cologne and then for a year at the Kennedy Institute in Berlin before moving to the newly established University of Bielefeld in 1971, where he remained until his retirement in 1996. He lectured throughout the world, in Japan, Britain, and Israel, and was a visiting professor at Harvard, Yale, Princeton, and Stanford, but Bielefeld remained the center of his professional and personal life. Here, together with his colleagues Jürgen Kocka and Reinhart Koselleck, he attracted an impressive number of talented young scholars who went on to have successful careers in Germany and abroad. Bielefeld's famous Friday afternoon colloquia, at which history faculty, students, and visiting scholars presented their work were always memorable—sometimes for the presenter, painfully memorable—occasions.

Few historians in any era have written so much, of such high quality, about so many different subjects. From his first book, published in 1962, until his last collection of essays, which appeared just a few weeks before his death, Wehler produced at least fifty books and hundreds of articles, reviews, and occasional pieces. Most of Wehler's work dealt with German history, and especially with the complex origins of what he continued to insist was Germany's exceptional path that ended with the disasters of Nazism. From very early on in his career, Wehler was interested in methodological problems, and particularly in the relationship between history and the social sciences, of which he was a well-informed if by no means uncritical admirer. His own research usually focused on the terrain where society and politics, wealth and power, interests and institutions intersect, the terrain that had been explored by Marx and Weber, who remained his intellectual heroes.

Wehler's doctoral dissertation was about German Social Democracy's views of nations and nationalism. While clearly inspired by Schieder's long-term interest in these issues, Wehler put them in a characteristically broad and original perspective, in part because he took the time to learn enough Polish to examine the Polish dimension of the national question. In what would be the first and last serious setback in an otherwise brilliantly successful career, the Cologne department rejected Wehler's Habilitation project on American imperialism. Eventually he published the results of his research in a series of important articles, which appeared in a collection entitled *Der Aufstieg des amerikanischen Imperialismus* (1974). For his Habilitation he turned to the vexing question of why, after steadfastly resisting colonial acquisitions, Bismarck suddenly took over several overseas territories in 1884. The result was a six-hundred-page study of *Bismarck und der Imperialismus* (1969), a powerfully argued and deeply researched analysis that attempted to uncover the domestic origins of Bismarckian foreign policy. In 1973, he published *Das Deutsche Kaiserreich*, a brief interpretative account of the German empire, based on lectures he delivered in Berlin and originally part of a series put out by Vandenhoeck and Ruprecht. This became the canonical statement of the so-called Sonderweg interpretation of German history; probably

Wehler's most widely read work, it has been translated into several languages, frequently cited, and intensely criticized. Although he continued to publish an uninterrupted series of articles and edited collections of essays, by the early 1980s more and more of Wehler's energies were directed to a single, monumental project, which would become a five-volume survey of German history from the beginning of the eighteenth century to 1990. *Deutsche Gesellschaftsgeschichte* (1987–2008) was based on decades of reading and reflection; it was a synthesis of the existing literature and a series of original, bold, and often-risky interpretations of particular problems. There is nothing quite like it in the scholarly literature and it is difficult to imagine that anyone will ever have the stamina, energy, and ambition to match it. Beautifully produced and skillfully marketed by Beck Verlag, the *Gesellschaftsgeschichte* sold remarkably well. The fifth volume was the subject of an online forum (the so-called Lesesaal), created by the *Frankfurter Allgemeine Zeitung*, in which for a period of several weeks a number of prominent commentators discussed the arguments and implications of Wehler's account.

In addition to his own work, Wehler was a tireless promoter of scholarship by others. His journal, *Geschichte und Gesellschaft* and the monograph series, *Kritische Studien zur Geschichtswissenschaft*, published some of the most significant new research especially about the social history of German politics. He also edited several important volumes designed to make social scientific concepts and methods accessible to the German historical profession, which he regarded, not unreasonably, as methodologically narrow and intellectually provincial. Wehler not only reached out to other disciplines, he turned back to the history of German historical scholarship for inspiration. His nine-volume series, *Deutsche Historiker*, was a collection of biographical sketches of historians, many of whom had been ignored or undervalued by the scholarly establishment and who, Wehler hoped, would provide models for a new generation.

Among those marginalized figures from Germany's past, no one was more important for Wehler's own intellectual formation than Eckart Kehr (1902–1933). Kehr, like Rosenberg, had been a student of Friedrich Meinecke's in Berlin during the 1920s, and had managed to produce a remarkable number of critical, politically engaged, and methodologically innovative studies before he died of a heart attack at thirty-one. Wehler's introduction to his edition of Kehr's essays, published as *Der Primat der Innenpolitik* (1965), at once praised Kehr's accomplishments and articulated Wehler's own scholarly agenda, which, like Kehr's, was to use a theoretically informed and empirically based study of the past in order "to hold up a critical mirror to the present." For half a century, this sense of mission nourished and directed Wehler's efforts as scholar, teacher, and commentator on public affairs.

Although Wehler never entirely lost the feeling of being something of an outsider, he became an academic and eventually a national celebrity. His reviews and commentaries appeared regularly in *Die Zeit* and *Der Spiegel*, he was frequently quoted and not infrequently attacked in the pages of the *Frankfurter Allgemeine Zeitung*, and was even the subject of a hilarious parody on Harald Schmidt's late-night comedy show (available on YouTube). As a public intellectual, Wehler intervened on a range of issues. Together with his lifelong friend, Jürgen Habermas, he played a major part in the so-called *Historikerstreit* of the 1980s. A decade later, he forcefully opposed Turkey's admission to the European Union, and, most recently, eloquently decried the growing inequalities of wealth and status in German society. Wehler retained the capacity to surprise and sometimes to outrage both his allies and opponents: for instance, while he was by no means an enthusiastic admirer of Roman Catholicism, he nevertheless came to the defense of Benedict XVI when the *Bild-Zeitung* attacked the pope's brief boyhood membership in the Hitler-

Jugend. ("I think that this entire controversy is grotesque," Wehler told *Der Spiegel*.)

In June 2012, the force of Wehler's public personality and the power of his presence were nicely captured by Ilse Stein, a reporter for the *Göttinger Tageblatt*. After enduring a seemingly endless series of speeches at a celebration of the 275th birthday of the University of Göttingen ("According to the invitation, the event was to be two hours long. Based on experience, it usually seems rather longer."), Stein describes the arrival on stage of the then eighty-year old historian, who was to deliver a Festrede entitled "Aufklärung in Göttingen im 18.Jahrhundert und heute": "After barely ten minutes, even the sleepiest attendees were wide awake, there was spontaneous applause, and in the back rows, the first discussions began. Wehler mastered the balancing act between remembering past Enlightenment scholars and addressing current questions of German politics." Here was Wehler at his very best— energetic, provocative, and articulate, engaging his audience with a subject that he made matter to them because it so clearly mattered to him. On that warm summer afternoon in Göttingen, as so often in his long career, Wehler represented the best traditions of enlightenment, learning, and political engagement.

Wehler was a vigorous, at times perhaps excessively vigorous polemicist, who deeply believed in the importance of uninhibited intellectual debate. His judgments of scholars with whom he disagreed were often harsh; he was not dismayed by their equally harsh responses. And while he was a resolute defender of his own views, he was rather more open to criticism than his public persona might suggest. A striking example of this openness is the fact that Thomas Nipperdey's incisive and deeply critical review of *Das Deutsche Kaiserreich* first appeared in *Geschichte und Gesellschaft*, Wehler's own journal. Wehler's ideas and interests changed significantly over time; among his strengths was the ability to adopt, defend, and then abandon concepts that he no longer found useful. The Wehler of the *Gesellschaftsgeschichte*, therefore, was a much more flexible and inclusive scholar than the author of *Das deutsche Kaiserreich*. But behind these changes remained a core of political convictions and epistemological values that sustained and guided his remarkable intellectual energy and scholarly commitment.

There was a private side of Uli Wehler that most people did not see. He could be a lot of fun to be around, a witty companion and gracious host. To scores of people throughout the world, he was an extraordinarily loyal and generous friend, who went out of his way to offer assistance and support. He was a proud and attentive father and an affectionate grandfather. Above all, he was a loving and devoted husband to Renate, who, for fifty-six years, was at his side in times of joy and sorrow. In a long lifetime graced by many blessings, she was the one he cherished most.

In 2004, Wehler concluded his moving memorial to his old friend Wolfgang Mommsen with these words: "There are many reasons to mourn the sudden loss of this extraordinary historian, who was for us a model of the liberal scholar, personifying the impressive fusion of scholarly erudition and political engagement." There are many reasons to mourn the passing of Hans-Ulrich Wehler, who died in Bielefeld, on 5 July 2014, still hard at work on a number of new projects and looking forward to debating the latest round of books on the origins of the First World War.

14

Gerhard A. Ritter[*]

Gerhard A. Ritter spent a productive decade (1964–1974) at the University of Münster and another two decades (1974–1994) in Munich, but he remained a Berliner. Born in 1929 in Moabit, he was reared in Dahlem, where he experienced the city's wartime devastation, occupation, and division. Soon after his retirement from his professorship in Munich, Ritter and his wife moved back to Berlin, where he became an active participant in the capital's cultural life and graciously entertained an unending parade of family, former students, and friends from near and far.

Ritter always stressed his modest background: both his grandmothers had worked as domestic servants, his father owned a small but successful publishing firm with close ties to the labor movement. Like every member of his generation, Ritter's life was shaped by the memories of National Socialism and the struggle to create a new, democratic Germany. As a doctoral student at the University of Berlin, he worked with Hans Herzfeld, who encouraged his critical engagement with the German past. Even more important for Ritter's intellectual development was the influence of Hans Rosenberg, who had

*Published in *Central European History*, 48, no. 4 (December 2015): pp. 458–60.

been forced to emigrate by the Nazis and returned to Berlin as a visiting professor in 1949 where he inspired an extraordinary constellation of future scholars (including, in addition to Ritter, Gilbert Ziebura, Gerhard Schulz, Wolfgang Sauer, Otto Büsch, Friedrich Zunkel, and Helga Grebing). Rosenberg's scholarly rigor, political commitment, and methodological range had an enormous impact on Ritter; the two men remained close, both intellectually and personally. Finally, Ritter was influenced by the two years he spent at St Antony's College in Oxford, where he established another important set of personal and intellectual connections with British scholars. Later in his career, Ritter was a visiting professor at Berkeley and Washington University in St. Louis, but for him, unlike for most of his contemporaries, Britain remained a more powerful presence than America.

Ritter's dissertation on the German labor movement at the end of nineteenth century (published by Colloquium Verlag in 1959 as *Die Arbeiterbewegung im Wilhelmischen Reich: Die Sozialdemokratische Partei und die Freien Gewerkschaften, 1890–1900*) was one of the first—and still one of the best—examples of what would become the new social history of politics. It was also the initial installment in Ritter's life-long engagement with the political and social history of German workers, which would produce a number of important books and essays, including Ritter's contribution to the multivolume series *Geschichte der Arbeiter und der Arbeiterbewegung seit dem Ende des 18. Jahrhunderts,* that was published by Dietz Verlag. The consistently high quality of this collective enterprise (which has now reached fifteen volumes) is a tribute to Ritter's skills as an editor and abiding influence as a scholarly model.

Ritter was a true comparativist, always alert to the interplay of similarity and difference that enriches our historical understanding. Comparative analysis, especially a comparison of Germany and Britain, was an important element in Ritter's longtime interest in the development of parliamentary institutions and political parties. An early expression of this was an extraordinarily imaginative essay on German and British parliamentarism, first published in 1962 and then in a revised version in *Arbeiterbewegung, Parteien und Parlamentarismus. Aufsätze zur deutschen Sozial- und Verfassungsgeschichte des 19. und 20. Jahrhunderts* (1976). Comparison also shaped Ritter's approach to another central theme of his scholarship, the origins and evolution of the welfare state. Here too he was a pioneer, defining a subject, providing foundational empirical research, and stimulating the work of others. His book on *Der Sozialstaat,* first published in 1989, then expanded and revised two years later, and translated into several languages, remains the best place to begin thinking about these fundamental issues of state formation.

As a Berliner who retained strong ties to the divided city, Ritter was more engaged by the momentous events of 1989 than many of his west German colleagues. He became actively involved in the commission that was responsible for the political and scholarly transformation of the Humboldt University, which turned out to be a difficult, demanding, and sometimes painful process. Characteristically, Ritter was inspired by the process of German unification to pose some important new historical questions, which he examined in *Der Preis der deutschen Einheit* (Beck, 2007, English translation from Oxford in 2011) and in his last monograph, *Hans-Dietrich Genscher, das Auswärtige Amt und die deutsche Vereinigung* (Beck, 2013).

In addition to his many works of scholarship and synthesis, Ritter was active as an editor, reviewer, and academic organizer. His source collections on social history, historical statistics, and voting behavior enriched the scholarly discourse and encouraged further research. He served on the editorial boards of several major journals and was actively involved in a number of important research projects on parliaments and parties, the German inflation, as well as the labor movement.

Prominent among Ritter's virtues was what the Romans would have recognized as *pietas*, a sense of duty and devotion to family and community, and particularly to one's ancestors. He wrote with great respect and affection about his teachers, especially Herzfeld and Rosenberg. Another expression of his filial piety was the time and effort he devoted to the collection of letters that he published in 2006, *Friedrich Meinecke. Akademischer Lehrer und emigrierte Schüler: Briefe und Aufzeichnungen, 1910–1977* (Oldenbourg, English translation from Brill in 2010), which documents three generations of German academics whose lives were shadowed by war, political repression, and exile. Ritter's final scholarly essay, in which he reflects on his relationship with German refugee historians in the United States, Britain, and Israel, will appear in *The Second Generation: Émigrés from Nazi Germany as Historians*, edited by Andreas Daum, Hartmut Lehmann, and James Sheehan. (Berghahn 2015).

Ritter was an extraordinarily successful teacher, a tireless editor and organizer of scholarly projects, and, perhaps most of all, a model of scholarly energy and engagement. There is a preliminary and necessarily incomplete record of Ritter's accomplishments in the Festschrift in honor of his sixty-fifth birthday edited by Jürgen Kocka, Hans-Jürgen Puhle, and Klaus Tenfelde, *Von der Arbeiterbewegung zum modernen Sozialstaat* (Saur, 1994). In the course of his long and productive career, Ritter received many honors, including the Prize from the Historisches Kolleg, honorary degrees from the University of Bielefeld and the Humboldt University, membership in the Bavarian Academy of Sciences, and the Bundesverdienstkreuz. From 1976 to 1980, he was president of the Deutscher Historikertag.

Although Ritter was never identified with a particular school or a single historical method, few historians in the postwar period had greater influence on the discipline. The source of this influence, I think, is what William James once called "temperament," by which he meant the complex blend of moral, psychological, and intellectual qualities that form our relationship to the world. Temperamentally, Gerhard Ritter was remarkably generous, open to new ideas, curious about every aspect of the past and engaged with the events of the present. He could be critical of other scholars, including— perhaps especially—of those he most admired, but he had the gift of criticizing without giving offense. This made him a wonderful mentor and a valuable friend.

Gerhard Ritter's wife Gisela died in 2013. Despite the usual infirmities of age, he remained active until the very last months of his life. He died on 20 June 2015, mourned by his two sons and their families, as well as by scores of friends and admirers from around the world.

15

Fritz Stern[*]

"You will lose everything you love most dearly; that is the arrow that Exile's bow will fire." With these words Dante begins his famous description of the pains of exile in Canto 17 of the Paradiso. For the Stern family—Dr. Rudolf Stern, his wife Käthe, and their two children, Toni and Fritz—the pains of exile began in September 1938, when, after some delay and with great reluctance, they decided that there was no place for them in Hitler's Germany. We can easily imagine the mixture of relief and anguish, expectation and sorrow, hope and anxiety which the Stern family must have felt as they left Breslau, the city in which they had lived and prospered. Fritz Stern chose to begin his memoirs, *Five Germanys I Have Known*, with a moving description of his return to Breslau (now Wrocław) forty years later, and thereby established the theme of exile and homecoming, loss and recovery, destruction and renewal that shaped not only this book but much of his life and work.

Fritz Stern entitled one of his collection of essays, *Zu Hause in der Ferne*, "at home far away," which was an appropriate

---

*A German version of this text was delivered to the Annual Meeting of the Orden Pour le Mèrite in Berlin, June 2017. It was published in the Orden's *Reden und Gedenkworte*, 43 (2015–2016/2016–2017): pp. 275–79.

sentiment for someone who was indeed at home in many distant places, especially in Sils Maria, to which he returned again and again, in Germany, and in the Netherlands. But he also had a genuine home, and that was of course New York City, where the Stern family settled after leaving Breslau and where, 78 years later, he died.

In April 1939, a few months after he arrived in New York, young Fritz, barely a teenager, felt sufficiently at ease in his new home that he wrote a letter, in somewhat awkward but absolutely correct English, to the city's mayor, Fiorello LaGuardia, urging him not to retire from public life—a precocious sign of Fritz's political engagement, sound judgment, and remarkable self-confidence. Except for a brief period teaching at Cornell and many trips to Europe, New York was home. And above all this meant Columbia University, with which, from 1943 when he enrolled as a freshman until 1997 when he retired as University Professor, his scholarly career and personal life were so intimately connected. Close by the campus was the Stern apartment on Claremont Ave., filled with books and furnished with the fine pieces that his family had managed to bring with them from Breslau. This was, I think, the place where Fritz felt most at ease because it was here that the various elements of his life came into balance. Die Ferne in dem Zuhause, "far away at home."

After briefly considering following his father's path into medicine, Fritz decided to study history, in part perhaps because of the inspiring teachers he encountered at Columbia, but mainly because he was convinced that history, and more specifically German history, could reveal the origins of the murderous regime from which his family, unlike so many others, had managed to escape. This was what he called "the burning question that I have spent my professional life trying to answer: why and how did the universal human potential for evil become an actuality in Germany?"

Stern's answers to this question changed over the course of his long career, but the question itself runs like a red thread through all of his writing, from his first book, *The Politics of Cultural Despair*, published in 1961, until his last, a collection of essays published in 2015.

"The historian must serve two masters, the past and the present." These words are from the introduction to Stern's first book, *The Varieties of History*, a collection of writings by historians about history that was published three years after he received his PhD, when he was just thirty years old. This was an astonishing debut by any standards, still in print and still unsurpassed as an introduction to the challenges and achievements of history as a discipline. Both the selections themselves and Stern's introduction revealed his temperament as a historian and intellectual, fully formed and vividly expressed as the very beginning of what would be a long and brilliant career. Here are the final lines of the introduction: when the historian studies the human past, "he touches on the ultimate questions of human existence. . . . And as he deals with men and their creations, he will alternately feel pride and exultation, awe and sorrow, at how varied, complex, unpredictable, wretched and glorious is human life."

In his lifelong efforts to grasp this wretchedness and glory, Fritz Stern worked best in what we can describe as a biographical mode. This was not because he shared Thomas Carlyle's conviction that "history was the biography of great men," but rather because he believed that historical forces and circumstances could best be seen in the lives of individuals as they struggled to shape, and were in turn shaped by, their historical world.

Stern's choice of subjects is worth noting. They include statesmen like Bismarck and Bethmann Hollweg, as well as influential intellectuals like Burckhardt and Nietzsche. But especially prominent among his subjects are two groups: one was German Jews, men like Bleichröder and Rathenau, who attempted to negotiate the pressures of assimilation and rejection that characterized the complex interaction of Jews and Germans, or exiles like Heine and Einstein, with whom Stern, for obvious reasons, felt a special affinity. The second group were members of the German resistance, most recently Dietrich Bonhoeffer and Hans von Dohnanyi, who were the subjects of a wonderful dual biography that he wrote with Elisabeth Sifton in 2013. These "no ordinary men" were important to Stern not only as small points of light in the dark night of the German past, but also as a source of hope for the future, the promise that Germans would have what he once called "Germany's second chance," a chance to reclaim its "squandered greatness."

Many of those who wrote about Fritz Stern's death noted that it marked the end of an era. And indeed he was among the last survivors of an important generation of public intellectuals who helped to shape the postwar world. But in remembering Fritz Stern we should not dwell too much on endings or on the past. Although he was a scholar devoted to understanding the past, he was also, like all great historians, alive to the possibilities of the present. He was what Raymond Aron called an "engaged observer," a link in a great tradition that the historian Gangolf Hübinger had recently traced from Max Weber to Fritz Stern's longtime friend and collaborator, Ralf Dahrendorf. Fritz Stern was a student of the past and a citizen of the present, but most of all he was someone who believed in the possibilities of the future. He never lost the capacity to hope for a better world, a world in which the values of freedom and human dignity would flourish. As husband, father, friend, scholar, teacher, and colleague, Fritz Stern has left us many gifts. Among them this capacity to hope is perhaps the one for which we should be most grateful because it is the one we need the most.

Conclusion

16

The Future of the German Past[*]

It is a truth universally acknowledged that our view of the past is shaped by our contemporary experience. "The historian," Fritz Stern once wrote, "must serve two masters, the present and the past."[1] But like so many universally acknowledged truths, this one turns out to be rather more complex than it initially appears. We know that the past is a vast storehouse filled with those imperfectly preserved relics of human experience with which we try to understand how people lived in another time and place. But what exactly is the present, that other master to whom we owe allegiance? The present, like Heraclitus's proverbial river, is inherently elusive, always changing, never still. Our idea of the present is also oddly elastic: when exactly does the contemporary era begin? 1945? 1989? Yesterday? In this regard, it is worth noting that five years from now, the historical period that began in 1945 will have lasted as long as the period between the creation of a unified Germany in 1871 and its destruction seventy-four years later. Although the title of these remarks refers to the past and the future, they are mainly concerned with the present, that is,

---

[*]A revised version of an essay published in *Central European History*, 51: Special Issue 1 (March 2018): pp. 159–63.
[1] Fritz Stern, *The Varieties of History* (New York, 1956), p. 32.

with those aspects of the contemporary world that might shape the way historians will view their subject in the years ahead.

Until recently, German historians' view of the past was not determined by the present in which they lived and worked, but rather by the shadow cast across the contemporary landscape by what we once agreed was "*the* German question," that is, the causes and consequences of National Socialism. Although the German question took many forms (its malleability was an important source of its persistence) and could evoke many different answers, it characteristically involved at least three assumptions. First, there was something distinctively German about Nazism. And therefore Nazism's connection to the German past and how it should be understood were debated by historians as they tried to plot this distinctive path, Germany's *Sonderweg*, towards catastrophe. Second, the most significant answers to the German question had to do with Germany's political failures. And once again, historians disagreed about the sources of this political pathology: was it, as the Bielefeld school insisted, an expression of social conflicts and class interests or, as their critics maintained, the result of Germany's distinctive geographical situation, or, as was particularly prominent among American scholars, the political consequences of Germany's cultural traditions. Most historians did agree, however, that politics was—and this is the third key assumption—national politics, that is, it concerned the political fate of the German nation created in 1871. As Hans-Ulrich Wehler once admitted, despite his generation's skepticism about nationalism and the nation state, "it was rare to transcend the analytical frame of national history."[2]

These three assumptions—the significance of the German question, the primacy of politics, and the centrality of the nation—provided the foundation for the master narrative of the German past that prevailed throughout much of the last

---

[2] Hans-Ulrich Wehler, *Notizen zur deutschen Geschichte* (Munich, 2007), p. 63.

half century. This narrative, while it has by no means disappeared, has lost much of its integrating power and authority.[3] As a result, German historians have become interested in a variety of new issues, open to the problems posed by contemporary politics, society, and culture, and increasingly engaged in a number of disconnected scholarly conversations.

There are symptoms of this disciplinary change all around us. One of them is the proliferation of articles (like this one) that raise questions about the future direction of German history.[4] Or consider an exemplary volume like *The Oxford Handbook of Modern German History*, edited by Helmut Walser Smith (2011), which covers many familiar themes but deliberately eschews a cohesive narrative structure.[5] The Fall 2017 issue of the *Bulletin of the German Historical Institute* featured a forum entitled "Diversity in German History," a celebration of different approaches to the past and a vivid reflection of the discipline's contemporary condition. And, to take one final example, the sessions sponsored by the Central European History Society at the American Historical Association's 2018

---

[3] On the origins and appeal of this master narrative, see James Sheehan, "Paradigm Lost? The Sonderweg Revisited," in Gunilla Budde, S. Conrad, and O. Janz, eds., *Transnationale Geschichte* (Göttingen, 2006), pp. 150–60.

[4] For the past decade, such articles, often in the form of reviews of recent works, have regularly appeared in *CEH* and in *German History*, the journal of the German History Society. See, for example, Andrew Port, "Central European History since 1989: Historiographical Trends and Post-Wende 'Turns'," *Central European History*, 58 (2015): pp. 238–48.

[5] See the Forum devoted to the *Handbook* in *German History*, 30, no. 2 (2012): pp. 247–64. I discuss the historiographical significance of the *Handbook* in a review essay for the *Archiv für Sozialgeschichte* (online), 53 (2013). Another example: Siegfried Weichlein's review essay on William Hagen's important synthesis, *German History in Modern Times* (2012), *German History*, 31, no. 2 (2013): pp. 239–44.

meeting represent a variety of subjects that fit within several different narrative frames.

One result of German historiography's present condition is the disappearance of those intense conflicts that erupted from the 1950s through the 1980s. The conventional view of postwar German historiography was given its canonical formulation by Georg Iggers, who stressed the discipline's agonistic nature, which was supposed to have originated in a struggle between a reactionary older generation (usually left unnamed, but presumably everybody knew who they were) and the advocates of a new, critical history, and was then elaborated in a series of debates, beginning with the controversy over Fritz Fischer's interpretation of the origins of the First World War and culminating in the *Historikerstreit* of the 1980s.[6] These debates were, of course, an expression of important differences among historians, some of them political (although the range of ideological diversity was, in fact, rather narrow), some methodological, and perhaps most important of all, some were what William James would have called "temperamental:" that is to say, differences in intellectual style and personality. But however deep and meaningful these differences sometimes appeared to be (especially to the participants themselves), it seems to me that German history was often so loud and contentious not because of what divided scholars, but because of how much they shared. It is precisely because the contestants share so much that family quarrels can be so bitter and prolonged. If there is a decline in contentious passion among contemporary German historians it is because we have less in common, not because our views about what matters have become more alike.

---

[6] Georg Iggers, *The Social History of Politics: Critical Perspectives in West German Historical Writing since 1945* (New York, 1985). For a good introduction to the *Historikerstreit*, see Charles Maier, *The Unmasterable Past: History, Holocaust, and German National Identity* (Cambridge, 1988).

An important reason for the erosion of historiographical consensus is a matter of institutional scale. Over the past half century, historiography's institutional setting has not fundamentally changed, but the discipline has expanded significantly; historical research is going on in more places, involving more people, and producing more material. Based on the listing of faculty in the AHA *Directory*, Catherine Epstein calculated that the number of American historians specializing in Germany increased from 201 in 1975 to 592 in 2010.[7] In Germany, disciplinary growth is even more striking. In 2005, Hans-Ulrich Wehler estimated that the number of history professors in Germany had gone from 170 to 1,300 over the past half century.[8] In 2016, the total number of full-time historians (including professors and other teachers and researchers) employed at German universities was 3,246—up from just over 2,000 ten years before. A significant aspect of this change in scale was the increasing number of women: female scholars were rare in the 1960s. In 2016, they made up more than a third of the historians at German universities, a number that had doubled over the preceding decade.[9] Demography is not destiny, but surely this expansion and diversification of the discipline has encouraged the pursuit of new topics and the adoption of new approaches.

Another important cause of disciplinary change is generational. From the 1960s through the 1980s, German historiography was shaped by scholars born around 1930. In Germany, this was the Hitler Youth generation, too young to

---

[7] Epstein, "German Historians at the Back of the Pack: Hiring Patterns in Modern European History, 1945–2010," *Central European History*, 56, no. 3 (September 2013): p. 601. The number of German specialists increased steadily until 2005 and then declined slightly five years later, suggesting that in the future there may well be fewer German historians (just as there will be fewer Germans).

[8] Wehler, *Notizen*, p. 92.

[9] *Statistisches Bundesamt, Fachserie* 11, Reihe 4.4 (2016), pp. 24 and 26.

have fought in the war, but old enough to have experienced the Third Reich and to have realized that, if it had lasted a little longer, they would have been actively involved.[10] In the United States and Britain, among the most prominent historians of Germany were members of the "second generation" of refugees, young people, almost all of them Jews, who had been born in Germany but were educated and then employed in their new homelands.[11] In both Germany and abroad, therefore, the traumatic impact of National Socialism gave this generation of scholars a distinctive sense of its historical identity and purpose. It is hard to find anything comparable for the generations that are now shaping German historiography. The two revolutionary events of the postwar era—1968 and 1989—lacked the integrating power of 1933 or 1945; the revolutions of 1968 and 1989 encouraged scholars to pose different questions, rather than inspiring them to seek different answers to the same question.

Both the German and American members of the generation born around 1930 had strong transatlantic ties. In Germany, this was the exchange-student generation. In America, most of the second generation established personal and professional links to Germany, often with the aid of the older generation of refugees—scholars like Hajo Holborn, Felix Gilbert, and Hans Rosenberg—who were their teachers, mentors, and senior colleagues. International connections remain of great importance for German historians—in fact, no other national historiography is as open to outsiders or has a stronger

---

[10] For an assessment of an exemplary member of this generation, see Paul Nolte's *Hans-Ulrich Wehler. Historiker und Zeitgenosse* (Munich, 2015).

[11] See Andreas Daum, Hartmut Lehmann, and James Sheehan, eds. *The Second Generation: Émigrés from Nazi Germany as Historians* (New York, 2016).

international presence.[12] But these cosmopolitan connections do not have the same ideological and personal power that they did for either the former exchange students or the second generation of refugees. Here again we confront the question of scale and diversity: the discipline's international ties have become wider and more extensive, but also more fragmentary and diffuse.

The primary characteristic of contemporary German historiography is its diversity. The German question remains important—National Socialism is still the most politically and morally fraught issue in modern European history. But the question has been reframed: historians are now less interested in the historical origins of Nazism—such as the weakness of German liberalism—than in the varied experiences of its victims and perpetrators and in the public and private memories of its crimes. One result of this is a shift in scholarly emphasis from the nineteenth to the twentieth centuries and from political to cultural and social history. The Holocaust remains what Andreas Wirsching called "the negative foundational myth" for postwar Europe, but historical research on the Holocaust, although more than ever the source of our persisting fascination with Nazism, has tended to drift away from a search for the German roots of mass murder and towards an exploration of the Holocaust's larger meaning for modern society, its transnational dimensions, and its distinctive place in Jewish history.[13]

---

[12] For example, at least twelve of the thirty-six contributors to the *Oxford Handbook of German History* do not teach in the country in which they were born.

[13] Wirsching, *Der Preis der Freiheit* (Munich, 2012), p. 385. The universal and particularistic dimensions of the Holocaust can be seen in the contrast between the two days on which it is commemorated, "International Holocaust Remembrance Day," January 27, established by the United Nations, and Yom HaShoah, marked in Israel a week after the end of Passover.

German history remains more dominated by political issues than many other national historiographies, but the meaning of politics has broadened, in part because contemporary political problems pose different dangers and offer different opportunities than those surrounding the German question. Moreover, German historians are now increasingly concerned with topics—popular culture, gender, sexuality, and emotions—that expand and sometimes transcend the conventional definition of politics and the usual chronological frame. Similarly, nations, nationalism, and national history have not gone away, but global, international, and comparative history are now much more important than twenty years ago. The history of regions, borderlands, and transnational connections has become more prominent, reflecting broader changes on the European scene. And, not surprisingly, historians' interest in issues like citizenship, identity, ethnicity, and emigration has taken on a new urgency, as Germany, like the rest of Europe, becomes an increasingly multi-ethnic society.

So far none of these approaches to German history—cultural history in all its various forms, transnational history, gender history—have provided the basis for a new consensus. Perhaps this is why we have trouble understanding how our view of the German past has been transformed. As Francis Bacon wrote at the beginning of the seventeenth century, "On waxen tablets you cannot write anything new until you rub out the old. With the mind it is not so; there you cannot rub out the old until you have written in the new." Thomas Kuhn had something similar in mind when he noted that scientific paradigms survive until they are replaced by something new, even if scholars are deeply aware of their limitations and internal contradictions.[14]

---

[14] Thomas Kuhn, *The Structure of Scientific Revolutions* (3rd ed., Chicago, 1996), p. 91.

We must consider the possibility that this situation is not, like Kuhn's paradigmatic crisis in the natural sciences, a transitional interlude, but rather a permanent condition. It may well be that no new consensus will emerge, that there will be no successor to the *Sonderweg,* the constantly contested but remarkably resilient grand narrative within which the postwar generation sought answers to the German question. Perhaps we should accept, even celebrate the fragmented diversity of contemporary scholarship and eagerly await those new questions that will compete for our attention. After all, the inexhaustible richness of its subject matter is among our discipline's most attractive attributes. That is why, as R. G. Collingwood once wrote, "The historian's work is never finished; every historical subject, like the course of historical events itself, is open at the end, and however hard you work at it, the end always remains open."[15]

---

[15] R. G. Collingwood, *An Essay on Metaphysics* (Oxford, 1939), p. 65.

Index

Abernethy, David, 2
Adenauer, Konrad, 146
Anderson, Margaret L., 100
Angress, Werner T., 6–7,
  149–52
Angress Family, 149–50, 152
Aron, Raymond, 168

Bacon, Francis, 178
Baring, Arnulf, 2
Barkin, Kenneth. 100
Beck Verlag. 147,156
Benedict XVI, 157–58
Berdahl, Robert, 41
Berlin, 3, 13–14
Berlin, Isaiah. 77
Bethmann Hollweg,
  Theobald von, 95, 167
Bismarck, Otto von, 12–
  13,21–24, 40–41, 49, 66,
  78, 86–90, 95, 111, 116,
  123, 146, 155, 167
Blackbourn, David, 101
Bleichröder, Gerson von,
  167
Bloom, Leopold, 75–77, 81
Boehme, Helmut, 35–36. 123
Bondy, Curt, 149

Bonhoeffer, Dietrich, 168
Boyen, Hermann von, 111
Braudel, Fernand, 19
Brel, Jacques, 3
Brecht, Bertolt, 45
Büsch, Otto, 161
Burckhardt, Jacob, 1, 45, 136,
  167
Butterfield, Herbert, 68–69,
  74

Camp Ritchie, 149–50
Carlyle, Thomas, 167
Catholicism, 2–3, 44, 100,
  157
Columbia University, 166
Craig, Gordon A., 12, 142–
  48
Custer, George Armstrong, 3

D-Day 1944, 150
Dahrendorf, Ralf, 96, 168
Dante, 165
Daum, Andreas, 163
Davidson, Donald, 4
Davin, Dan, 144, 148
De Maistre, Joseph, 42
Dickens, Charles, 146

Dilthey, Wilhelm, 111, 148
Dohnanyi, Hans von, 168
Droysen, J. G., 63–67, 111,
   113

Eichhorn, Karl Friedrich,
   133
Eichmann, Adolf, 3
Einstein, Albert, 168
Elections in Germany, 41, n.
   33
Eley, Geoff, 101
Emigrés, Jewish, 6, 9–10,
   109–16, 153–54, 175–76
Engels, Friedrich, 36
Epstein, Catherine, 175
Epstein, Klaus, 154
European Union, 104
Exchange Students, German,
   10–11, 98, 153, 176

Fay, Sidney, 145
Febvre, Lucien, 71
Federal Republic of
   Germany, 50, 79–91
Fehrenbach, Elizabeth, 67
Feldman, Gerald, 124
Ficker, Julius von, 65–66
Fischer, Fritz, 95–97, 99, 174
Fontane, Theodor, 144, 147
Fox, Edward Whiting, 31
Frankfurter Allgemeine Zeitung,
   156–57
Franz, Eugen, 35–36
Frederick II of Prussia, 80,
   86
Freud, Sigmund, 45
Freytag, Gustav, 37, 57–58

Friedländer, Saul, 139–41
Frisch, Max, 45
Frost, Robert, 133

Geary, Dick, 48
Gellner, Ernest, 60
Gerhard, Dietrich, 112–13
German Democratic
   Republic, 13, 79–91
German language, 5–6
"German Question," 10–11,
   147, 166–67, 172
German Unification, 1866–
   1871, 20–21, 24, 32, 35,
   41–42, 66–68
German Unification, 1989–
   1991, 14, 84–85, 102, 162
Gerschenkron, Alexander, 94
Gervinus, Georg, 65–66
Geyer, Michael, 103–4
Giesebrecht, Wilhelm von,
   65
Gilbert, Felix, 9, 111–15. 176
Goethe, J. W. von, 19, 30
Gollwitzer, Heinz, 136
Goubert, Pierre, 47
Grebing, Helga, 161
Grillparzer, Franz, 70
Grimm, Jacob, 57, 59–62,
   133

Habermas, Jürgen, 86, 97,
   157
Häusser, Ludwig, 67
Haffner, Sebastian, 112
Halcomb (Craig), Phyllis. 144
Haller, Johannes, 58
Hauptstadt debate, 15, 84–85

Haym, Rudolf, 113
Hazlitt, William, 146
Hegel, G. W. F., 133, 135
Heimpel, Hermann, 51–52, 72–73
Heine, Heinrich, 20, 93, 168
Henderson, W. O., 34–36
Heraclitus, 171
Herder, J. G., 55–56, 58–61, 77, 92
Herzfeld, Hans, 160, 163
Hintze, Otto, 61, 113, 119
Historikerstreit, 174
Hitler, Adolf, 12–13, 95, 130, 139
Hitler Youth, 10, 98, 153, 157, 175
Holborn, Hajo, 94–95, 97, 114, 176
Hollinger, David, 73
Holocaust Commemorations, 177, n. 13
Holy Roman Empire, 26–27, 27, n. 12, 131–32
House of History, 82
Hübinger, Gangolf, 168

Iggers, Georg, 99, 174

James, William, 163, 174
Jarausch, Konrad, 103–5
Joyce, James, 2, 76, 90
Justi, Johann, 133

Kaelble, Hartmut, 126, 136
Kafka, Franz, 45
Kaiser, Philip, 144

Kehr, Eckart, 99, 117–28, 157
Kierkegaard, Søren, 15
Kocka, Jürgen, 101, 154, 163
Koselleck, Reinhart, 121–22, 154
Krieger, Leonard, 59
Kuhn, Thomas, 106, 178–79

Laband, Paul, 123
LaGuardia, Fiorello, 166
Lamprecht, Karl, 68
Langer, William, 146
Langewiesche, Dieter, 104
LeBras, Hervé, 73
Lefebvre, Georges   , 33
Lehmann, Hartmut, 163
Lerche, Peter, 82
Luther, Martin, 29, 80

Mann, Klaus, 113
Mann, Thomas, 93
Mannheim, Karl, 115–16, 120
Marx, Karl, 93, 155
Meinecke, Friedrich, 8, 58, 67–68, 109–16, 157
Metternich, Klemens von, 25
Meyrink, Gustav, 140
Mommsen, Wolfgang, 159
Morsey, Rudolf, 123
Mumford, Lewis, 85
Museum for German History, 79

Napoleon, 64–65
NATO, 104

Nietzsche, Friedrich, 44, 52, 158, 167

Nipperdey, Thomas, 100

Nonn, Christoph, 154

Osterhammel, Jürgen, 103–5

Ostpolitik, 13

Oxford University, 143, 161

Plessner, Helmuth, 94

Pocock, John, 53,68, 73, 79

Pollard, Sydney, 70

Princeton University, 142–45

Puhle, Hans-Jürgen, 126, 163

Puttkamer, Robert von, 122, 127

Quad, Matthias, 19

Raabe, Wilhelm, 37

Ranke, Leopold von, 19–20, 57–59, 62, 65, 111

Rathenau, Walther, 167

Renan, Ernest, 51

Ritter, Gerhard, 58

Ritter, Gerhard A., 109–16, 160–64

Rosenberg, Hans, 8–9, 94–95, 97, 99, 113–14, 121–22 153–54 157, 160, 163, 176

Rostow, W. W., 144

Saint Ignatius High School, 2–3

Sauer, Wolfgang. 161

Savigny, Friedrich Carl, 56–57, 59, 61, 133

Schieder, Theodor, 47, n. 47, 49, 154–55

Schiller, Friedrich, 19, 30

Schlegel, Friedrich, 53

Schloss, Hohenzollern, 86

Schmidt, Harald, 157

Schmoller, Gustav von, 68, 109–11

Schorske, Carl, 8, 135–38

Schmitt, Bernadotte, 146

Schulz, Gustav, 161

Sifton, Elisabeth, 168

Smith, Helmut Walser, 173

Social Democratic Party (SPD), 9, 44, 48, 135–37

Socialist Unity Party (SED), 79

Sombart, Werner, 93

Sonderweg, 11–12, 90, 92–106, 129, 131, 155, 172, 179

Sontag, Raymond J., 7, 135, 144–45, 150

Srbik, Heinrich von, 63, 67

Stalin Note (1952), 86

Stanford University, 3–4, 12

Stein, Ilse, 158

Stein, Karl Freiherr vom, 120–21

Stern, Fritz, 120–21, 154, 165–68, 171

Stern Family, 165

Sternberg, Dolf, 82

Stürmer, Michael, 83

Sumner, B. H., 143

Sybel, Heinrich von, 57–59, 65–67

Tacitus, 55
Tenfelde, Klaus, 163
Thibaut, Anton, 61
Tilly, Richard, 36
Tipton, Frank, 33, 70
Tirpitz, Alfred von, 124–25, 127
Tocqueville, Alexis de, 3
Todd, Emmanuel, 73
Treitschke, Heinrich von, 20–22, 66, 123
Troeltsch, Ernst, 111

Ulysses, 75–77, 90
University of California at Berkeley, 5–7, 135–38

Vatican Council, 2
Veblen, Thorstein, 93–94
Vischer, Theodor, 109–11

Wagner, Richard, 44
Waitz, Georg, 61
Walker, Mack, 39, 129–34

Walser, Martin, 83
Weber, Eugen, 41
Weber, Max, 109–11, 155, 168
Wehler, Hans-Ulrich, 96–101, 118, 153–59, 172, 175
Whig Interpretation of English History, 68–69
Wilson, Woodrow, 143
Wirsching, Andreas, 177
Wittgenstein, Ludwig, 97
Wodehouse, P. G., 146
Wolf, Eric, 42–43
Woodward, C. Vann, 33
Woodward, E. L., 143
Wright, Gordon, 4
Wrigley, E. A., 47, 70

Ziebura, Gilbert, 161
Ziekursch, Johannes, 33
Zollverein, 34–36, 42
Zunkel, Friedrich, 161